Earth-Friendly WEARABLES

The Earth-Friendly Series

Earth-Friendly Toys

How to Make Fabulous Toys and Games
from Reusable Objects

Earth-Friendly Wearables

How to Make Fabulous Clothes and Accessories
from Reusable Objects

How to Make Fabulous Clothes and Accessories
from Reusable Objects

George Pfiffner

John Wiley & Sons, Inc.

New York • Chichester • Brisbane • Toronto • Singapore

The publisher and the author have made every reasonable effort to ensure that the experiments and activities in this book are safe when conducted as instructed but assume no responsibility for any damage caused or sustained while performing the experiments or activities in the book. Parents, guardians, and/or teachers should supervise young readers who undertake the experiments and activities in this book.

Library of Congress Cataloging-in-Publication

Pfiffner, George, 1923-
    Earth-friendly wearables : how to make fabulous clothes and accessories from reusable objects / George Pfiffner.
        p.   cm.
    — (the earth-friendly series)
    Includes bibliographical references.
    ISBN 0-471-00823-0 (paper : acid-free paper)
    1. Juvenile literature. 3. Recycling (Waste, etc.)—
Juvenile literature. [1. Dress Accessories. 2. Handicraft.
 3. Recycling (Waste)] I. Title. II. Series.
TT560.P45 1995
646.4'8—dc20 94-27482

Printed in the United States of America
10 9 8 7 6 5 4 3 2 1

Produced for John Wiley & Sons, Inc.
by Tenth Avenue Editions, Inc.
Creative Director: Clive Giboire
Assistant Editor: Matthew Moore
Editorial Assistants: Gene Aguilera, Dema Mantooth, Dennis Myers, Judy Myers, Andrew Razza, Bettina Rosner, and Peter Wagner
Artist: George Pfiffner
Assistant Artist: James Immes
Photographs: George Roos
Models: Kevin Gilmartin, Tracy Groves, Ashley Nemeth, Danny Nemeth, Mark McHie, Sheena McHie, Jason Rios, Melissa Valenzuela

Foreword

Every day when we open our mail at the Environmental Action Coalition, we find letters from young people all over the country. We have probably received a letter from your town, maybe even from your school.

Sometimes the letters ask questions, such as "How can we start a recycling program?" or "How does a landfill work?"

Sometimes they report on recycling projects kids have started, such as "We use both sides of our notebook paper" and "Our Boy Scout troop collected 392,000 cans."

We are always glad to get letters like these because we have been working on recycling since 1970, when only a few people were involved. Today people are coming up with more and more ideas about recycling.

Young people have made a big difference. You have come up with new ideas. Many of you have started recycling programs in your schools. You have taught your parents and grandparents how important recycling is, so the whole family can help keep the environment clean.

This is a very important moment in the history of the environmental movement. Young people all over the world are working together to try to save our planet from being buried under garbage.

As you can see from the globe on the cover of this book, you are part of an international movement. We all have a lot to learn from each other.

Have you heard the slogan *Reduce*, *Reuse*, and *Recycle*? These three simple words will give you the key to taking environmental action.

Reduce the amount of garbage you create. This means telling the person in the store that you don't need a bag to carry what you bought.

Reuse means finding a new life for something instead of throwing it away. That's what this book is all about.

Recycle means taking used materials and making them into materials that can be used again. Like turning old newspaper into newspaper that can be printed on again.

Whether you are already an active recycler or are just getting started, this new series of books will give you many projects that you and your friends can make using things that would otherwise be thrown away.

If you enjoy the projects in this book, the next step is to show your friends how to make them.

You might also come up with some of your own ideas for projects. If you do, I'm sure the publisher would like to hear about them, so write them down. Who knows, maybe they'll be in the next book.

If you like the idea of recycling stuff, then you can look into what kind of recycling program your community has, or you can start a recycling program in your school. Ask your teacher for help.

But now it's time to get out your scissors and pencils and paste so you can get to work. Have a great time!

Steve Richardson
Executive Director,
Environmental Action Coalition

Contents

Being Earth-Friendly, 9

Getting Started, 10

Methods, 11

STUFF FOR YOUR HEAD

Renewed Beret, 19

Yarn Headband, 21

Ear Decorations, 25

Scrunchie, 29

Sun Hat, 33

Baseball Cap, 37

Tiara, 43

Sunglasses, 47

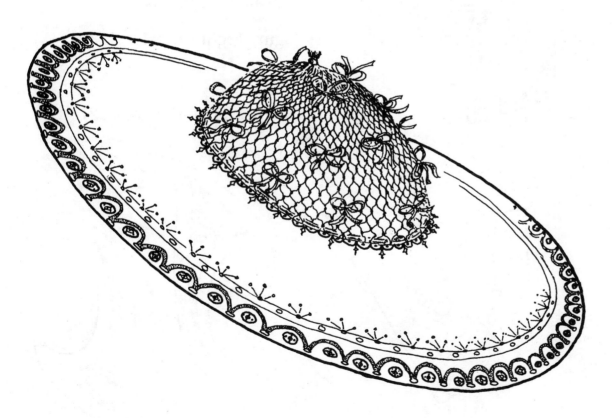

TOPS AND THINGS

Bottle-Cap Badge, 53

Vest, 55

Paper Necklace, 57

Coin Necklace, 61

Patches, 65

Layered Tops, 71

Bandanna Shirt, 75

Bar-Code Pin, 79

Foil Necklace, 83

BELTS AND BAGS

Cloth-Covered Belt, 89

Yarn Belt, 93

Tote Bag, 97

Plastic-Bag Belt, 101

STUFF FOR YOUR HANDS AND FEET

Spiral Bracelet, 107

Rings, 109

Fancy Shoelaces, 111

Four Bracelets, 115

Cloth Fingernails, 119

Mosaic Fingernails, 121

Figure-Eight Bracelet, 123

Staying Earth-Friendly, 127

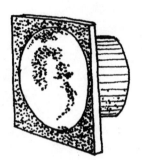

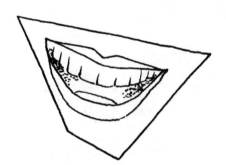

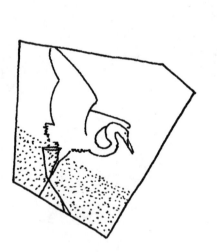

Being Earth-Friendly

Across the country and around the world, people are learning to reduce, reuse, and recycle. We have only one Earth, so we need to learn how to take care of it. We need to learn how to be "Earth-friendly."

Some people think that recycling is just about washing out cans and tying up newspapers. But we think that recycling is really about re-thinking—seeing the things around you in a new way.

When you start thinking about things in a new way, you can see that what used to be a toilet-paper tube is now a bracelet; what used to be an old pair of jeans is now a tote bag. This book, and the other books in this series, are about using your imagination to make new things out of old "trash."

There are 28 wearables for you to make in this book. Every wearable is made out of already-used materials. As you learn how to make cool fashions, you will also be learning about how to help the environment. We've included information about recycling, and tips on how you can help.

But the most important thing about this book is that it's fun! Every project in this book is fun to do, and the fashions you make are fun to wear. Even when you've made all the wearables in this book, the skills and ideas are yours forever—who knows where your imagination will lead you.

Getting Started

Your projects will be much easier if you follow all the instructions carefully. Here are some tips to get you started.

Before You Do Anything
Read all of the instructions and look at the drawings **before** you start making a project. The more you know about how the project is made, the easier it will be to follow the steps.

Level of Difficulty
Each project is rated according to how easy it is to complete. Here's a key to the symbols used to rate each project:

 = quick and easy

 = little time and medium difficulty

 = time consuming and challenging

You might want to start with some of the easier and faster projects until you get the hang of following the instructions.

Work Time
Set aside plenty of time to work on each project, and give it your full attention. Your wearables will turn out better if you don't hurry, and if you aren't distracted.

Work Place
After choosing a wearable to make, decide on the best place to work. Some projects require more space than others. For example, you will need a flat surface to make the Vest, but only for a few minutes. For the Mosaic Fingernails you will need to leave the project someplace safe over night.

Materials
Get together everything you will need for the project before you start. Put all the tools and materials on or near your work surface so that you can find them easily while you are working.

Some materials are easy to find at home. For some projects you will have to collect the materials you need. Don't be discouraged if you don't have exactly the materials we suggest. In many of the projects you can substitute materials. Ask your parents to help you decide if a substitute will work.

Recycling Facts and Tips
Some projects have Recycling Facts and Tips at the end. These are ideas about how you can re-think and recycle every day.

Symbols You Will Need to Know

! Steps marked with an **!** need to be done with an **adult helper**. If you don't have an adult to help you, don't try this project.

✪ **Even Better:** Indicates ideas about how to make your wearables more interesting.

Have Fun!

Methods

The methods on the next few pages are shortcuts that are used in many of the projects. You may want to try them out before you start working on your first wearable.

The Transfer Method will help you transfer patterns from this book onto cardboard and cloth.

The Threading Method will help you thread needles, which can be tricky.

The Whip Stitch Method shows you how to sew cloth together with a simple stitch.

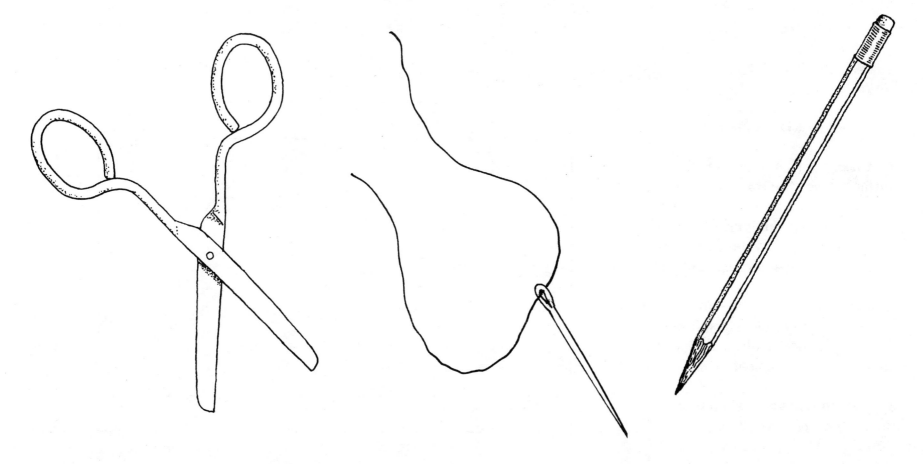

The Transfer Method

For some of the projects in this book you will need to transfer patterns from the book to paper, cardboard, or cloth. This method will make that easy to do.

You Need

- ❏ a hard pencil
- ❏ a pencil sharpener
- ❏ a soft pencil
- ❏ tape
- ❏ tracing paper

Instructions

1. Working on a smooth, level surface, place the tracing paper over the design or pattern you want to transfer. Tape all four corners of the tracing paper to the pattern to keep the tracing paper from moving.

2. Trace the lines of the pattern onto the tracing paper using a soft pencil. Sharpen the pencil often so that the lines are clear and neat.

3. When you have finished tracing the pattern, remove the tape and turn the tracing paper over.

4. Use a soft pencil to cover all the lines on the back side with pencil shading. Use the side of the pencil lead to make the shading.

5. Turn the tracing back over and tape it onto the surface you've selected for the pattern. Transfer the pattern to that surface by retracing over the lines, this time with the hard pencil.

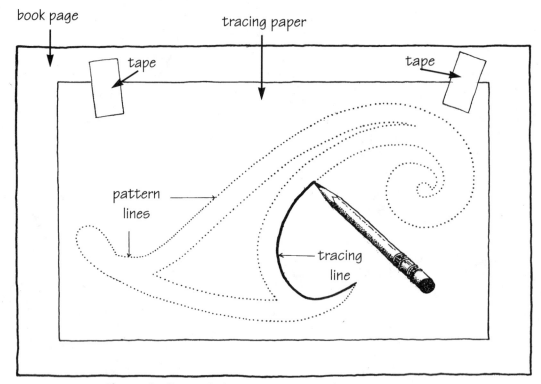

book page   tracing paper   tape   tape

pattern lines

tracing line

Trace the lines of the pattern onto the tracing paper.

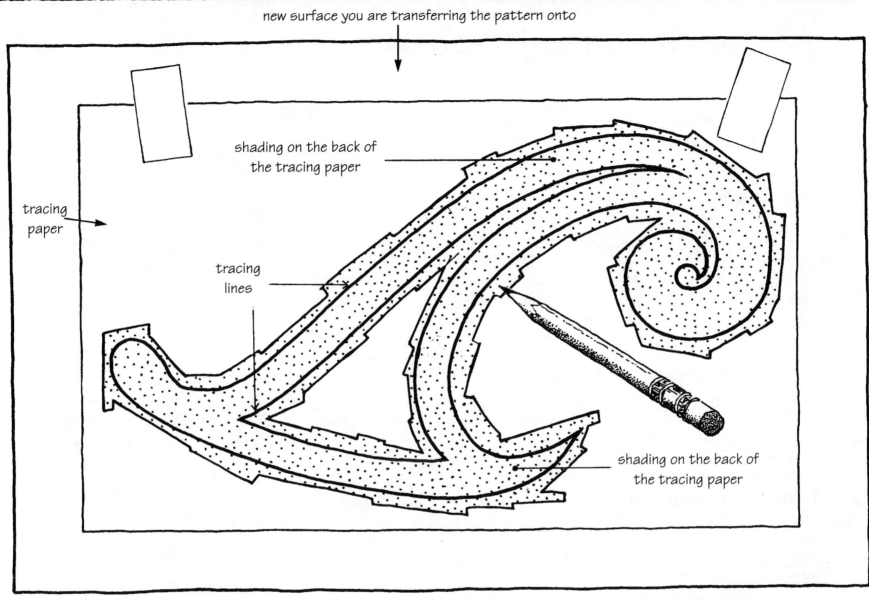

new surface you are transferring the pattern onto

shading on the back of the tracing paper

tracing paper

tracing lines

shading on the back of the tracing paper

To transfer the pattern, draw over your tracing lines with a hard pencil.

6. You can lift up a corner of the tracing paper to check that the pattern is being transferred clearly. If it isn't, add more shading with the soft pencil.

7. When the entire pattern has been transferred, you may want to darken the lines with a pencil.

The Threading Method

Threading a needle can be difficult. It will be easier if you follow these simple steps.

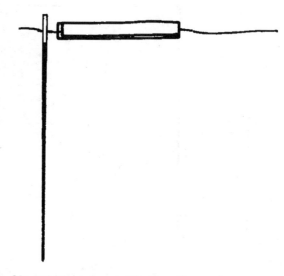

You Need

- ❑ a needle with a large eye
- ❑ a small piece of paper
- ❑ thread

Instructions

1. Tie a knot in one end of the thread.

2. Wet the opposite end of the thread and twist it tight.

3. Fold a small piece of paper in half, as shown below. The piece of paper needs to be small enough to fit through the eye of your needle when folded in half.

4. Open the paper and lay the unknotted end of the thread along the fold line.

5. Refold the paper over the thread.

6. Slip the paper with the thread through the eye of the needle. Remove the paper and pull a little more thread through the needle.

The Whip Stitch Method

The whip stitch is used to join the edges of two pieces of fabric in a seam, as in the Bandana Shirt, the Tote Bag, and other projects. You can also use the whip stitch to attach the Patches to fabric.

You Need

❑ a threaded needle

Instructions

1. Make sure the thread has a knot in one end.

2. Line up the edges of the fabric so that they are even. Pin the edges together with straight pins.

3. Push the needle through both pieces of fabric near the edges of the fabric. Pull the thread through the fabric until it is stopped by the knot.

4. Loop the thread over the edge, and push the needle up through the cloth again, about ¼ inch (.6 cm) away from the first stitch, making sure that the needle always comes through the cloth in the same direction.

5. Repeat along the length of the joined edges.

6. When you have sewn along the entire edge, tie a knot around the last stitch and cut the thread.

7. Remove the straight pins.

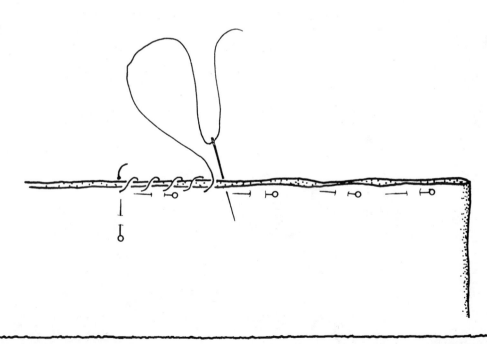

Stuff for Your Head

Renewed Beret

Brightly colored ribbons turn an old beret into
something special. This hat can be worn in any season,
and is sure to make you the talk of the town.

You Need

- ❑ one old beret
- ❑ ¾ inch × 4 feet (2 × 120 cm) of gift-wrap ribbon

Tools

- ❑ a pencil
- ❑ a ruler
- ❑ scissors

Instructions

1. Use the scissors to cut two rows of slits in the beret, as shown in the diagram. The first row of slits should be roughly 1 inch (2.5 cm) up from the hat band. Make one pair of slits that go in the same direction as the hat band. Make the next pair of slits pointing from top to bottom. Keep going around the beret until you have come back to the first pair of slits. The slits in each pair should be about ¼ inch (0.6 cm) apart.

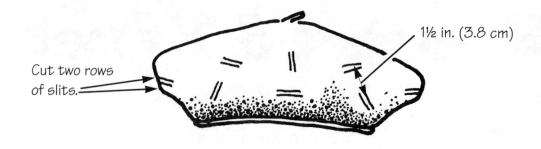

Cut two rows of slits.

1½ in. (3.8 cm)

2. The second row of slits should be about 1½ inches (3.8 cm) up from the first row. The slits in the second row should point in the opposite direction from the matching pair of slits in the first row, as shown above.

3. Cut the ribbon into two 2-foot (60-cm) pieces.

4. Pull one ribbon section most of the way through one pair in the first row of slits.

5. Weave the ribbon through all the pairs of slits in the first row, so that you end where you started. Twist the ribbon once between each pair of slits.

6. You can leave the ends of the ribbon loose, or you can tuck them into a pair of slits, so the ends are inside the beret.

7. Thread the second ribbon through the second row of slits in the same way.

8. Your beret is ready to wear!

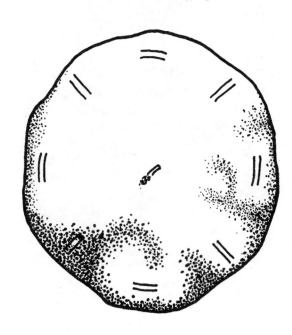

top view

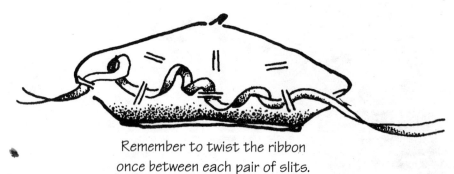

Remember to twist the ribbon once between each pair of slits.

Yarn Headband

A little leftover yarn can quickly become a cool headband.
This is the perfect thing to make with friends on a rainy day.

You Need

- ❏ yarn in two colors
  (10 feet [3 m] in all)

Have on Hand

- ❏ paper
- ❏ a pencil
- ❏ a piece of stiff cardboard
  (such as the back of a pad
  of paper)

Tools

- ❏ a 30-inch (75-cm) piece
  of string
- ❏ a ruler
- ❏ scissors

Instructions

1. To measure your head:

a. Wrap the string once around your head where you would wear a headband.

b. Pinch the string where it overlaps. Make a mark where you have pinched the string.

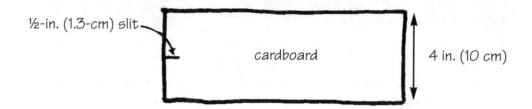

½-in. (1.3-cm) slit

cardboard

4 in. (10 cm)

c. Use the ruler to measure the distance from the end of the string to the point you marked.

d. Divide this measurement in half and write down the number. For example, if your head measured 20 inches (50 cm), half of that is 10 inches (25 cm).

2. Cut a piece of cardboard that is the length you found in step **1d** and at least 4 inches (10 cm) wide.

3. Use the scissors to cut a ½-inch (1.3-cm) -deep slit in the middle of one end of the cardboard.

4. Make a knot at the end of one color of yarn. Slip the yarn into the slit so that the knot is pushed up against the cardboard.

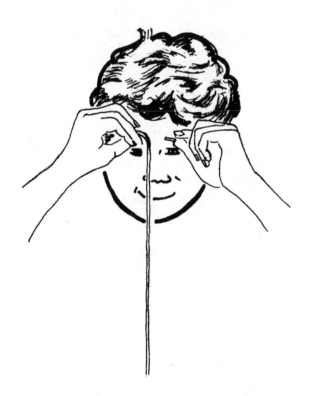

Slip the yarn into the slit against the knot.

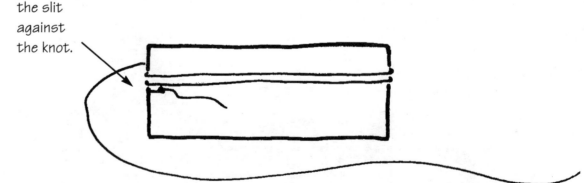

5. Wrap the yarn around the cardboard the long way 12 times. Make the wraps just tight enough to keep the yarn in place. Do not pull the yarn tight.

6. Cut the yarn. Tie the end to the end of the second color yarn.

7. To wrap the second color of yarn:

    a. Wrap the second yarn twice **around** the 12 wraps of the first yarn on one side of the cardboard.

    b. Turn the cardboard over. Wrap the yarn twice around the first yarn on the other side.

    c. Do this about 12 times on each side, keeping your wraps bunched together as shown.

8. Tie the remaining end of the second color to the end of the first color yarn and cut off any extra yarn.

9. Remove the headband from the cardboard and put it on your head.

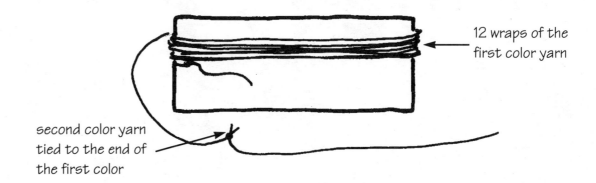

12 wraps of the first color yarn

second color yarn tied to the end of the first color

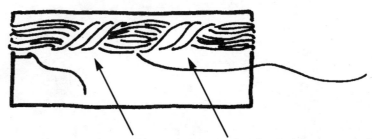

Wrap the second color twice around the first color on each side of the cardboard.

Tie these ends together after you wrap the second color yarn.

Ear Decorations

Far-out ear decorations can be made from cardboard and foil. You can be the height of earthly style or a visitor from another planet!

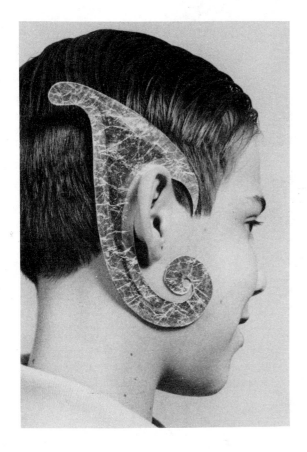

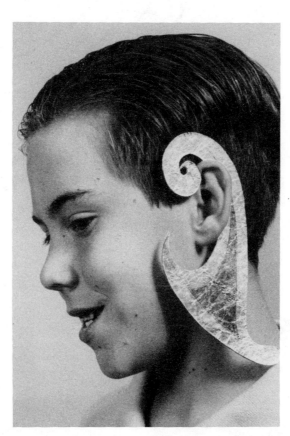

You Need

- ☐ three large pieces of light cardboard (such as from a cereal box)
- ☐ four pieces of silver or gold foil (such as from chocolate bars)

Have on Hand

- ☐ a fine-tip pen
- ☐ permanent marking pens
- ☐ stick glue

Tools

- ☐ a hole punch
- ☐ scissors

Instructions

1. Copy the Ear Decoration Pattern to one piece of cardboard using the Transfer Method (see page 12).

2. Cut out the pattern, including the inside section. Use the hole punch to punch a hole in the top of the pattern, as shown.

3. Use the pattern and the pencil to trace the outline only of the ear decoration onto another piece of cardboard.

4. Cut out the outline.

5. Repeat steps **3** and **4** to make a second ear decoration.

6. Crumple the foil slightly; then carefully smooth it out with your fingers.

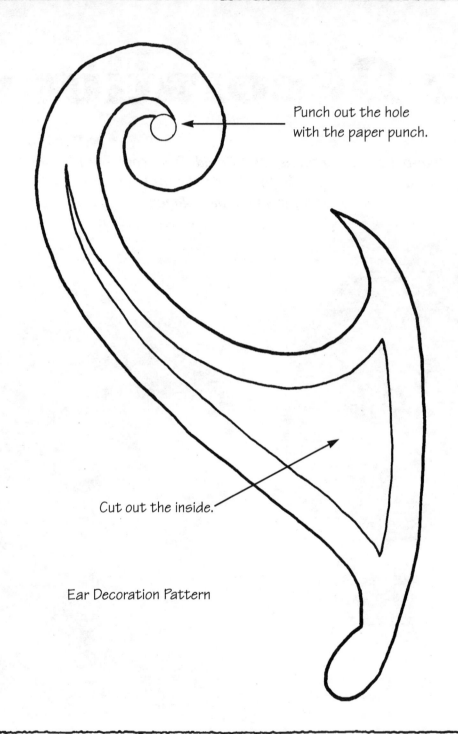

Punch out the hole with the paper punch.

Cut out the inside.

Ear Decoration Pattern

7. Apply stick glue to both the cardboard and the back of the foil. Place the foil on the cardboard and smooth the foil down carefully around the ear decoration.

8. Trim the foil along the edges.

9. Repeat steps **6–8** to cover the back of the first decoration and both sides of the second decoration.

10. Place the pattern on top of one of the foil-covered pieces. Line up the edges. Trace along the inside edges of the pattern with the fine-tip pen. Repeat on the other side.

11. Fill in these outlines with a colored marking pen.

12. Repeat on the second decoration.

13. Hook the ear decorations over your ears. You can wear the ear decorations with either end up, and with either side out, so each one can be worn four ways.

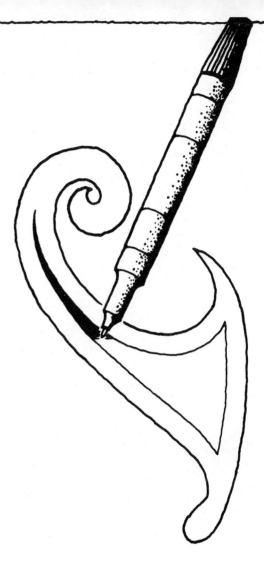

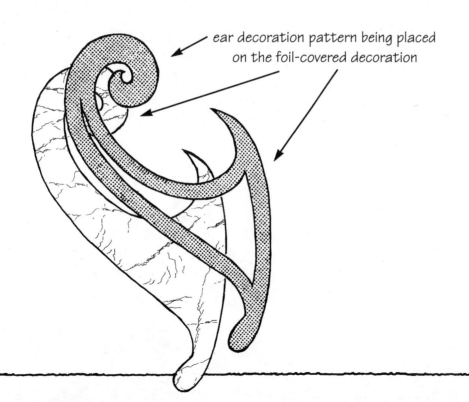

ear decoration pattern being placed on the foil-covered decoration

✪ **Even Better:** Make ear decorations with friends and you can start a trend.

Scrunchie

Scrap fabric can become the perfect thing to keep your hair back with style. This scrunchie is so easy to make, you may want a different one for every day of the week.

You Need

- ❏ two 4-inch (10-cm) rubber bands
- ❏ one 5 × 10-inch (12.5 × 25-cm) piece of scrap fabric

Have on Hand

- ❏ a needle
- ❏ straight pins
- ❏ string
- ❏ thread

Tools

- ❏ scissors
- ❏ stick glue

Instructions

1. Place the fabric face down on your work surface.

2. Apply stick glue along the ends of the short sides of the back of the fabric.

3. Fold the ends of the short sides over, and glue them to the back of the fabric to make a hem.

4. Fold the fabric in half lengthwise, with the back side facing out.

5. Line up the long edges of the fabric and pin them together.

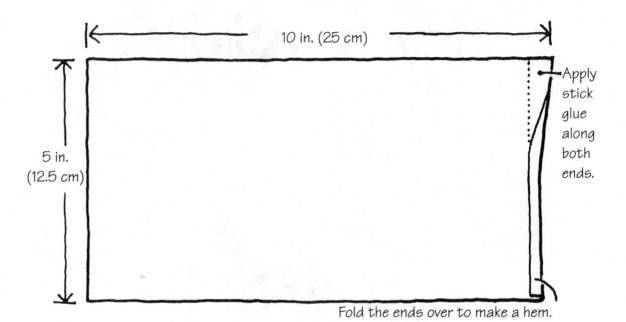

10 in. (25 cm)

5 in. (12.5 cm)

Apply stick glue along both ends.

Fold the ends over to make a hem.

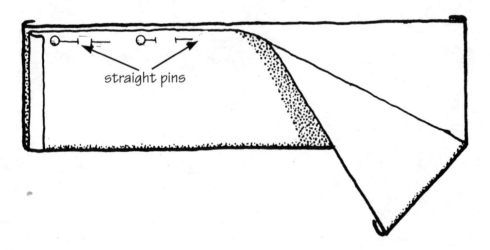

straight pins

6. Sew the long edges together ¼ inch (.6 cm) from the edge using the Whip Stitch Method (see page 15). Remove the pins as you sew.

7. Turn the cloth right side out.

Tying the Rubber Bands Together

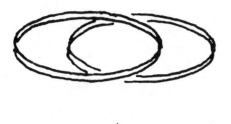

1

2

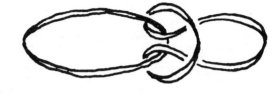

3

8. Tie the rubber bands together using the method shown above: Place one rubber band on top of the other and pull one end of the bottom rubber band through and over the top rubber band and through the center of itself. Pull the rubber bands tight.

9. Push the rubber bands through the middle of the tube of cloth.

10. Tie the loose ends of the rubber bands together with a piece of string.

11. Line up the open ends of the fabric. Pin the ends together.

12. Sew the ends together using the Whip Stitch Method (see page 15) and remove the pins.

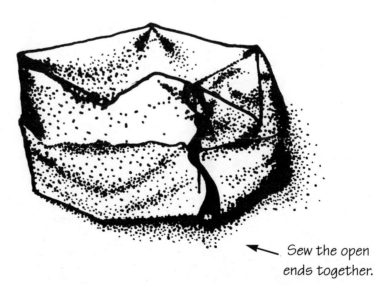

Sew the open ends together.

Sun Hat

Make a hat that's perfect for tea parties or
masquerades, or just to keep the sun out of your eyes.
This fashionable head covering reuses a plastic sack and a pizza box.

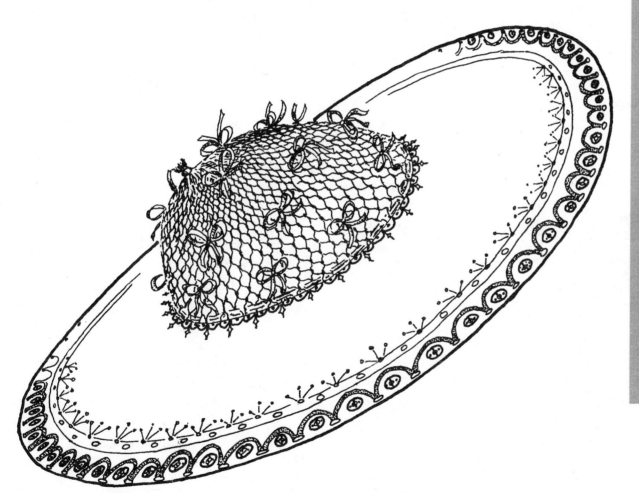

You Need

- one plastic-mesh sack (such as an onion sack)
- two 18-inch (45-cm) squares of cardboard (such as from a pizza box)
- ribbon

Have on Hand

- glue
- marking pens
- plastic food wrap

Tools

- a compass (for drawing circles)
- masking tape
- a pencil
- a ruler
- scissors

Instructions

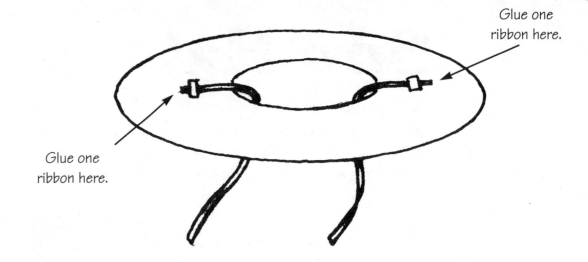

Glue one ribbon here.

Glue one ribbon here.

1. To make the crown:

a. Pull the mesh sack over the top of your head.

b. Pinch the sack with your fingers, just above one ear.

c. Take the sack off your head and weave a pencil into the spot you pinched.

d. Cut the sack all around, 1½ inches (3.8 cm) below the pencil.

Note: It's easier to cut the sack if you lay it flat.

e. Make 1½-inch (3.8-cm) cuts into the sack, 1 inch (2.5 cm) apart, all the way around the bottom, so that you make tabs.

2. To make the brim:

a. With the ruler and pencil, draw two diagonal lines (from corner to corner) across the cardboard.

b. Place the pivot of the compass where the diagonal lines cross. Draw the biggest circle the compass can make.

c. Draw a circle with a 4¼-inch (10.6-cm) radius from the same point.

d. Repeat steps **a–c** with the second piece of cardboard.

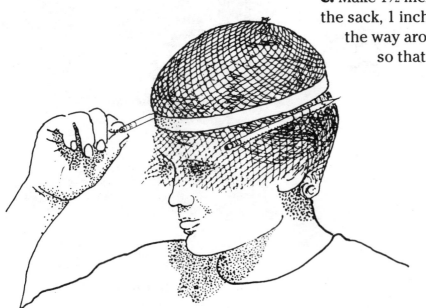

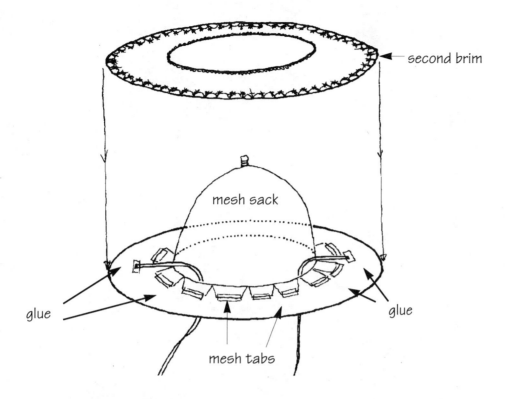

second brim

mesh sack

glue

mesh tabs

glue

6. Place a piece of plastic wrap over the tabs.

7. Place the brim on a flat surface with small weights (bottles, books, cans) on top of the plastic while the glue dries. When the glue is dry, remove the weights and peel off the plastic.

8. Decorate one side of the second brim with marking pens.

9. Trail glue around the hole and outside edge of the brim with the mesh crown attached. Keep the glue at least 1 inch (2.5 cm) away from each edge.

10. With the decorated side up, press the second brim down onto the first. Be careful to align the edges. Wipe away any glue that oozes out. Put some books on the brims to keep them flat until they dry.

✪ **Even Better:** Decorate the crown by tying bows of ribbon into the mesh.

e. Cut out both circles with the scissors. Save the cut-out circles.

f. Try on the brims together. If the inner hole is too small for your head, replace the cut-out circles and mark a larger circle in the middle. Cut out the new circle and try the brims on again.

3. Cut two pieces of ribbon about 18 inches (45 cm) long. Glue 3 inches (7.5 cm) of each ribbon onto opposite sides of one of the brims, as shown on the opposite page.

4. Place the mesh tabs over the hole in the same brim. Secure each tab with a short piece of masking tape.

5. Squeeze trails of glue over the mesh tabs.

Baseball Cap

Take the field with a cap made from cardboard, cloth, and a plastic-mesh bag. Score one for recycling with this fun hat!

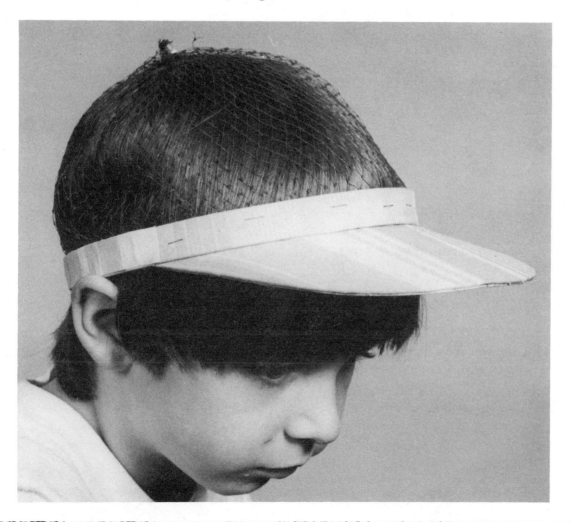

You Need

- ❑ light cardboard (such as from a large cereal box or pizza carton)
- ❑ scrap fabric, 12 × 24 inches (30 × 60 cm)
- ❑ a plastic-mesh bag (such as onions come in)

Have on Hand

- ❑ masking tape
- ❑ paper clips, 1 dozen
- ❑ stick glue
- ❑ yellow glue (also known as "wood glue")

Tools

- ❑ a pushpin
- ❑ a ruler
- ❑ scissors
- ❑ a stapler
- ❑ two pencils

Instructions

1. To make the visor:

a. Transfer the Visor Pattern and the Visor Fabric Pattern (page 42) onto cardboard using the Transfer Method (see page 12).

b. Cut out the patterns with scissors. Be sure to cut along the tab lines shown on the patterns. Score the dotted line by scratching the cardboard with a pushpin.

c. Trace the cardboard Visor Fabric Pattern onto the fabric. Be sure to mark the tabs shown on the pattern. Label this piece of fabric A.

d. Trace the cardboard Visor Pattern onto the fabric, without the tabs. Label this piece of fabric B.

e. Cut both pieces out of the fabric with scissors. Be sure to cut all the tab lines.

f. Apply stick glue to the back of piece A and to one side of the cardboard. Smooth the fabric onto the cardboard.

g. Glue the fabric tabs that stick out over the edge to the other side of the cardboard.

h. Apply stick glue to piece B and to the other side of the cardboard.

i. Smooth the fabric onto the cardboard.

2. To make the headband:

a. Measure around your head, where you will wear the headband, with a piece of string.

b. Use the scissors to cut a piece of cardboard $5/8$ inch (1.6 cm) wide and as long as your head measurement plus $1/2$ inch (1.3 cm). Label this piece C.

c. Cut a second piece of cardboard that is the same width and just slightly shorter than the first piece. Label this piece D. Put this piece aside to use later.

d. Cut a third piece of cardboard that is the same width and 4 inches (10 cm) long. Label this piece E.

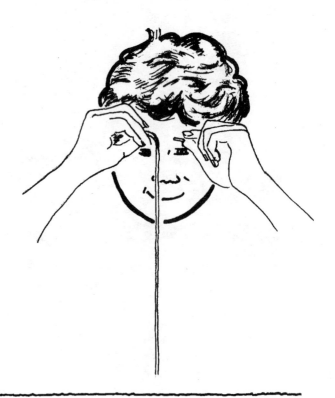

e. Use the scissors to cut one piece of fabric 1$\frac{1}{8}$ inches (2.9 cm) wide and the length of the longest cardboard strip (piece C).

f. Apply stick glue along piece C. Apply glue to the back of the fabric you have just cut. Glue the fabric to the cardboard. Fold the flaps over the edge and glue them to the other side of the cardboard.

g. Apply yellow glue to one side of piece E.

h. Apply yellow glue to the back of piece C, at the ends. Carefully bend piece C into a circle, with the fabric on the outside.

i. Glue piece E onto the back of piece C, to keep the ends of C together. Use paper clips to keep the pieces in place.

j. Let the glue dry for 30 minutes. Remove the paper clips.

3. To attach the mesh:

    a. Put the mesh bag on your head.

    b. Slip the headband over the mesh bag to where you will wear the headband.

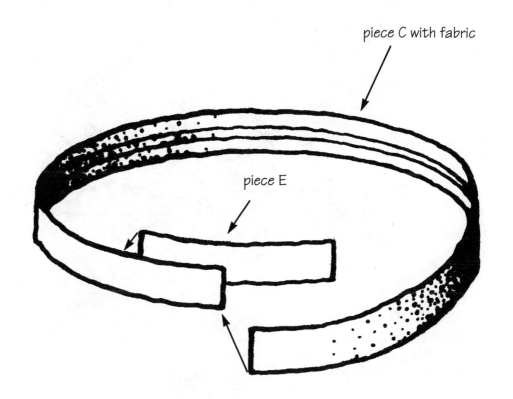

piece C with fabric

piece E

c. Weave a pencil through the mesh just below the headband. Weave a second pencil through the mesh on the opposite side.

d. Carefully remove the headband and mesh.

e. Use the scissors to cut around the mesh, on the line made by the pencils.

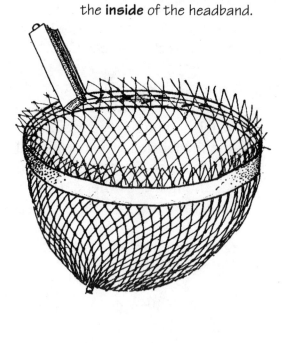

Staple the mesh crown to the **inside** of the headband.

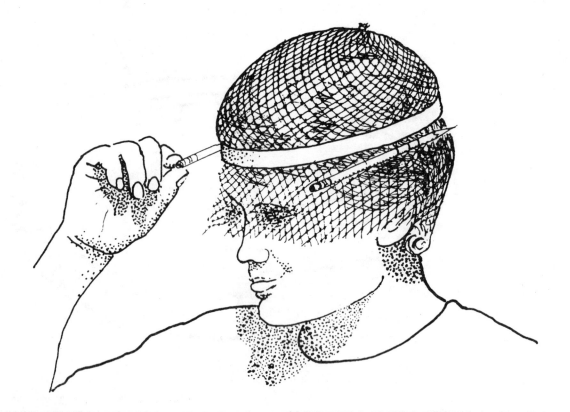

f. Use the stapler to attach the mesh crown to the inside of the headband. Staple from the outside every 1 inch (2.5 cm) along the headband. Be sure to catch the mesh with each staple.

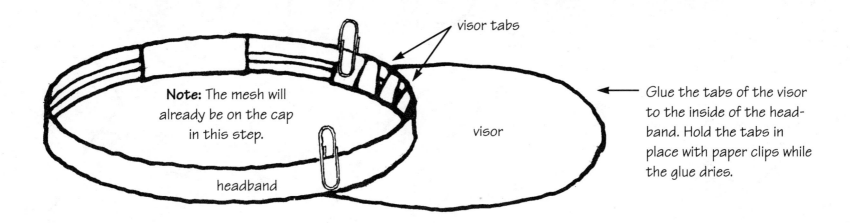

visor tabs

Note: The mesh will already be on the cap in this step.

visor

headband

Glue the tabs of the visor to the inside of the headband. Hold the tabs in place with paper clips while the glue dries.

g. Bend the tabs of the visor and glue them to the inside of the headband. Hold the tabs in place with paper clips. Let the glue dry for at least 20 minutes before going on to the next step.

h. Put yellow glue on cardboard piece D.

i. Glue cardboard piece D along the inside of the headband. Use the paper clips to keep it in place. Let the glue dry for two hours, and your baseball cap is done.

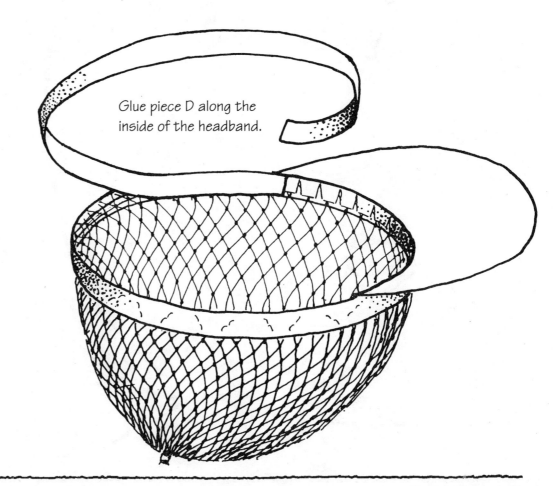

Glue piece D along the inside of the headband.

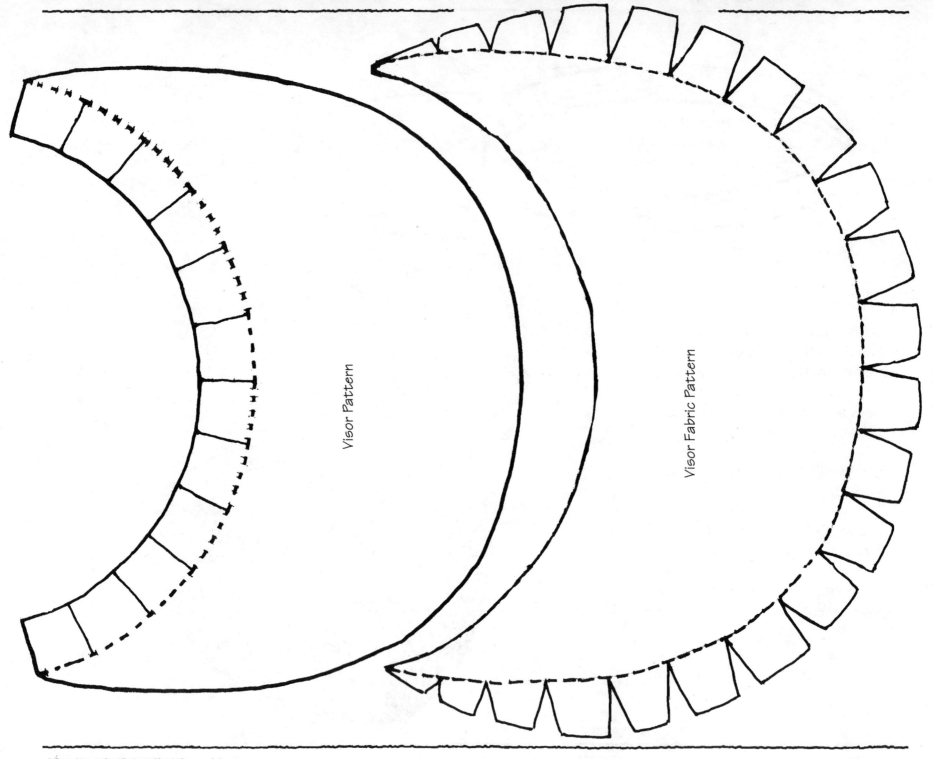

Visor Pattern

Visor Fabric Pattern

Tiara

*You can be royalty in this recycled crown
made from a plastic take-out container.*

Instructions

1. Wash and dry the plastic container. Cut the container in half along the hinge. You will only need half the container, so be sure to recycle the other half.

2. Cut the lid in half diagonally (from corner to corner). Again, you will only use one half, so be sure to recycle the other half.

You **must** use this kind of plastic container.

Cut the lid in half diagonally.

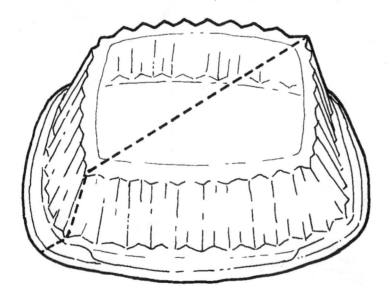

3. Place the lid flat side down on the Tiara Pattern on page 45. Use the marking pen to trace the curved line onto the plastic.

4. Use the scissors to cut along the line you have just marked.

5. Use the hole punch to punch a hole in each side of the tiara, as shown on page 45.

6. Measure and cut two 10-inch (25-cm) -long pieces of string.

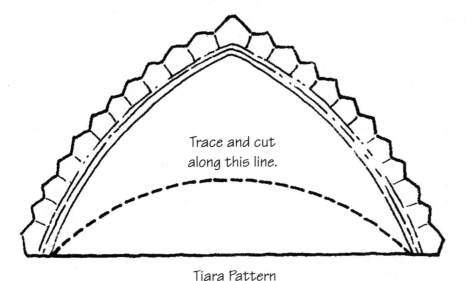

Trace and cut along this line.

Tiara Pattern

7. Tie one end of each string to one of the holes you punched in step **5**.

8. Tie the tiara onto your head, with the strings going around the back of your head.

✪ **Even Better:** You can decorate your tiara any way you want—with markers, poster paint, or glued-on shapes or pictures. Go wild!

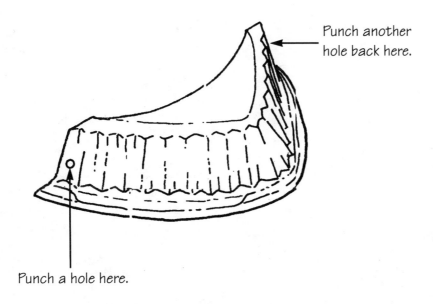

Punch another hole back here.

Punch a hole here.

Sunglasses

These keep-cool shades, cut from just a piece of scrap cardboard, make the perfect disguise. No one will know it's you behind these recycled shades.

You Need

❑ light cardboard (such as from a cookie or cereal box)

Have on Hand

❑ a black marker
❑ a heavy book
❑ stick glue

Tools

❑ a pencil
❑ a ruler
❑ scissors

Instructions

1. Transfer the Shades Pattern to a piece of cardboard using the Transfer Method (see page 12). Use a ruler to keep the slits straight and even.

2. Cut out the pattern. Be especially careful when you are cutting out the slits.

3. Transfer the Earpiece Pattern two times onto a piece of cardboard.

4. Transfer the Hinge Pattern two times onto a piece of cardboard.

5. Cut out the earpieces and hinges.

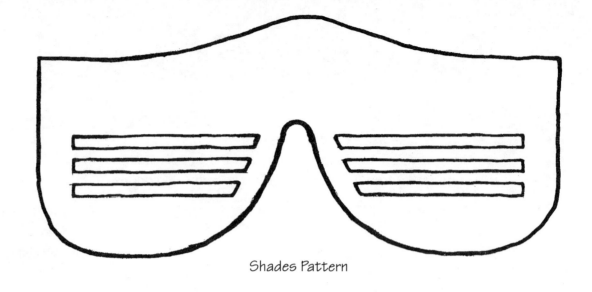

Shades Pattern

Hinge Pattern (Make two.)

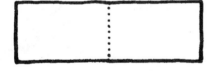

6. Use the marker to color all the pieces black.

7. Carefully fold the hinges in half. Be sure to score along the fold line before you fold. To "score," run the

tip of the scissors down the line without cutting through the cardboard, to make the cardboard easier to fold.

8. Apply stick glue to one side of each hinge, and to a spot on the end of each earpiece opposite the notch.

Earpiece Pattern

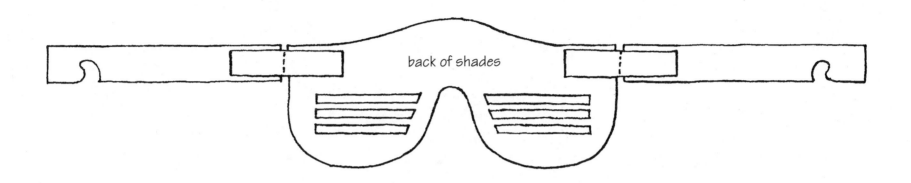

back of shades

9. Glue one half of each hinge to each earpiece. Make sure that the edges are lined up.

10. Apply stick glue to the upper corners of the back of the shades, as shown. Glue the hinges to the back of the shades. Make sure that the tops of the shades and the hinges line up.

11. Lay the shades out flat on your work surface. Place a heavy book on top of the shades and the earpieces for an hour to flatten them out.

12. Put your shades on and take a look around.

✪ Even Better: If the shades don't fit tightly enough, you can attach a piece of string or a rubber band to the holes on the ends of the earpieces.

WARNING: Do not use these shades when you need to be on the alert, like when you are bicycling or in-line skating.

Tops and Things

Bottle-Cap Badge

*You can make a badge that's funny, pretty, scary, or far-out
from a bottle cap, cardboard, and a magazine picture.
Make a badge to suit yourself or give it as a gift.*

You Need

- ❏ a picture cut from a magazine
- ❏ a piece of cardboard slightly larger than the picture
- ❏ a plastic bottle cap

Have on Hand

- ❏ black poster paint
- ❏ glue
- ❏ a paintbrush
- ❏ scrap cardboard

Tools

- ❏ scissors

Instructions

1. Cut out a picture that you like from a magazine.

2. Paint the back of the picture with black poster paint. Leave the paint to dry for 20 minutes before going to the next step.

3. Coat the back of the cutout and one side of the cardboard with glue and stick them together. Wait at least 20 minutes for the glue to dry. While you wait, go on to the next step.

4. To make the plug to hold the badge in place, cut a round piece of scrap cardboard that is just a little smaller than the bottle cap:

    a. Place the bottle cap down on the scrap cardboard. Mark around it.

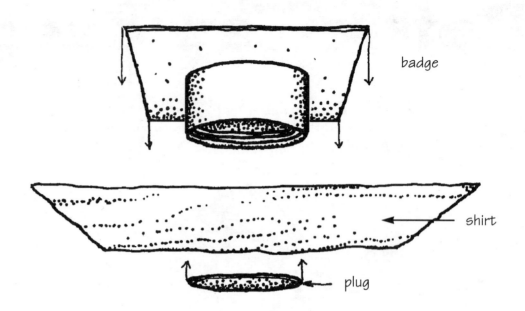

badge

shirt

plug

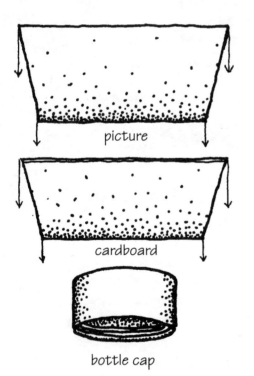

picture

cardboard

bottle cap

b. Use scissors to cut around the marked circle. Be careful to cut along the inside of the circle so that it is slightly smaller than the bottle cap.

5. Once the glue is dry, trim the extra cardboard from around the cutout.

6. Glue the back of the cutout/cardboard to the top of the bottle cap. Be sure that the bottle cap is in the center of the cutout/cardboard. Set this aside to dry for 20 minutes.

7. When the badge is finished, you can attach it to your shirt by putting the badge on one side and pushing the plug through the cloth into the bottom of the bottle cap.

✪ **Even Better:** You can make the badge last longer by brushing glue on the front of the picture. This will prevent warping and scratches.

Vest

When a shirt you love is worn out, you can make it into a vest in five minutes. This is as fun to make as it is to wear.

You Need

❑ one button-front shirt

Have on Hand

❑ straight pins

Tools

❑ a pencil
❑ a ruler
❑ scissors

Instructions

1. Button the shirt.

2. Neatly spread out the shirt on its back on the floor.

3. Cut off both sleeves.

4. Turn the collar straight up. Cut the collar off where it joins the shirt.

Cut here.

tered between the buttons and the right side seam, as shown in the diagram.

c. Make a mark 2 inches (5 cm) below the bottom button.

d. Use scissors to make curved cuts connecting these three points, as shown in the diagram. Be sure to cut through the front of the shirt only.

e. Repeat on the left side.

5. Make a curved cut down from the collar hole on one side to just above the fourth button up from the bottom.

6. Repeat on the other side.

7. To finish the bottom:

a. Make a mark on the right side seam that is roughly even with the bottom button.

b. Make a mark about halfway up between the bottom edge of the shirt and the bottom button, cen-

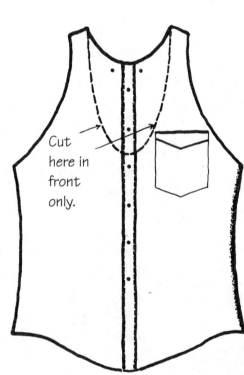

Cut here in front only.

Cut along the dashed lines.

2 in. (5 cm)

Mark here.   Mark here.

f. Turn the shirt over. Cut off the shirttail straight across, connecting the marks on the left and right side seams.

Paper Necklace

Here's a project that makes a necklace out of yesterday's news. You'll be up to date and in fashion at the same time.

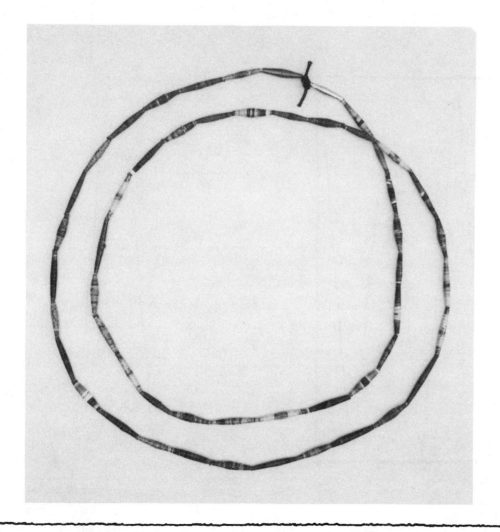

You Need

- four colorful pages cut from magazines
- dark ribbon or string; no more than ⅛ inch thick and about 5 feet long (.3 cm × 1.5 m)

Have on Hand

- plastic wrap
- a small dish or a used jar lid
- stick glue
- white glue

Tools

- a glue brush
- a pencil
- round toothpicks
- a ruler
- scissors

Instructions

1. Use the ruler and pencil to make marks every 1½ inches (4 cm) along one long edge of one magazine page.

2. Do the same on the opposite edge of the page, but start ¾ inch (2 cm) from the edge.

3. Use the ruler to connect the marks, as shown in the Bead Diagram below.

4. Cut along the lines. Discard the two half-pieces on the ends.

5. Roll one piece tightly onto a round toothpick, starting at the wide end. Apply stick glue to the underside of the last 2 inches (5 cm) of paper before rolling it into place. (Note: If you can't roll the paper onto a toothpick, use a pencil instead.)

Bead Diagram

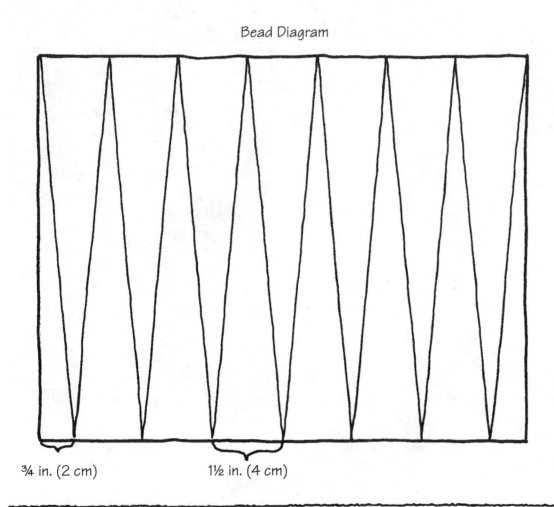

¾ in. (2 cm)   1½ in. (4 cm)

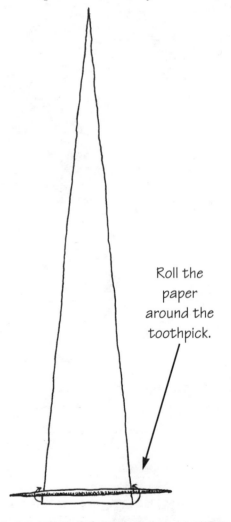

Roll the paper around the toothpick.

6. Let the glue dry for a minute. Then carefully pull the toothpick out from inside the rolled paper. The rolled paper is now one bead for your necklace.

Carefully pull the toothpick out from inside the rolled paper.

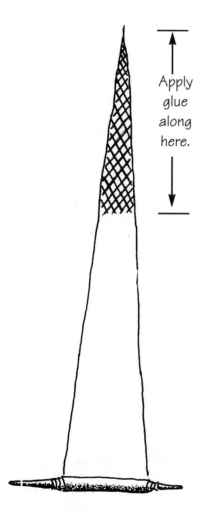

Apply glue along here.

7. Repeat steps **5** and **6** to make the rest of the beads.

8. Make a glue "varnish" by mixing white glue with several drops of water in a jar lid.

9. Use the glue brush to coat each bead with the glue "varnish." Set the beads on a piece of plastic wrap to dry.

10. Dip the ends of the string into white glue to stiffen them. Wipe off any extra glue and pull the ends straight. Dangle the ends off the edge of a table so that they do not touch anything while drying (about 20 minutes).

11. When the string ends are dry, thread the beads onto the string.

12. Tie the ends of the string together. Use scissors to trim off any extra string.

13. Put your necklace on.

✪ **Even Better:** If you want, you can paint the beads in your necklace, or decorate them with markers.

Coin Necklace

You can look like you're dripping with money with the help of a few aluminum pie pans. This necklace can be worn to the opera or just around the house.

You Need

- one old, disposable, aluminum pie pan, 8 inches (20 cm) in diameter or larger, cleaned and dried
- four or five coins of different sizes (larger than a nickel)
- a piece of light cardboard (such as from a cereal box)
- two pieces of cord or gift-wrap ribbon about 1/8 inch (0.3 cm) wide, one 10 inches (25 cm) long and the second 48 inches (1.2 m) long.

Have on Hand

- facial tissue
- stick glue
- transparent tape
- white glue

Tools

- a pencil with a blunt point
- a pencil with a sharp point
- scissors
- a spoon

Instructions

1. Cut the bottom out of the pie pan. Be very careful of any sharp edges.

2. Tape the faces of the coins to one side of the aluminum. Make sure that the coins are more than ½ inch (1.3 cm) away from each other. Turn the aluminum over.

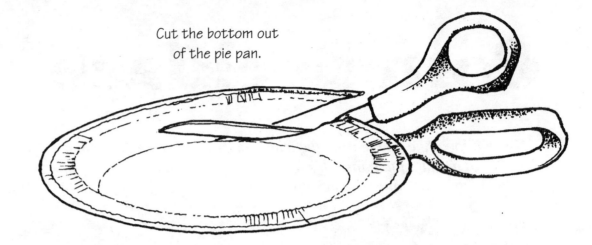

Cut the bottom out of the pie pan.

3. Rub over each of the coins with a spoon handle. Keep rubbing until the outline of each coin appears.

4. Rub the blunt pencil point over each coin. Continue rubbing until the coin images are clear. Be sure to include the edges.

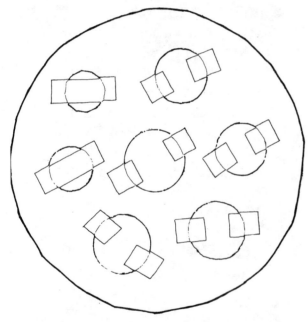

coins taped to the aluminum

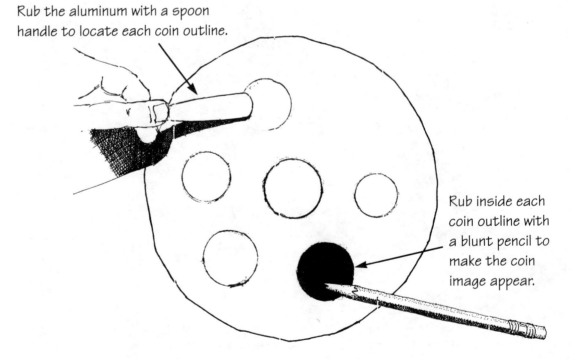

Rub the aluminum with a spoon handle to locate each coin outline.

Rub inside each coin outline with a blunt pencil to make the coin image appear.

5. Wipe away the pencil marks with a tissue.

6. Untape the coins from the aluminum.

7. Carefully cut out the coin images from the aluminum.

8. Place the original coins on the light cardboard. Use a sharp pencil to draw around each coin.

9. Cut out the cardboard disks with scissors.

10. Apply a heavy amount of stick glue to the cardboard disks and a little to the back of the aluminum coins. Gently stick the cardboard onto the back of the aluminum.

11. Lay the phony coins face down on your work surface, about 1/8 inch (0.3 cm) apart. Make sure that the tops of the coins are all pointing away from you, and that the centers of the coins are all in a line. Use tape to hold the coins in position.

12. Place a dab of glue just below the center of each coin.

coins taped to cardboard with cord taped over the backs of the coin

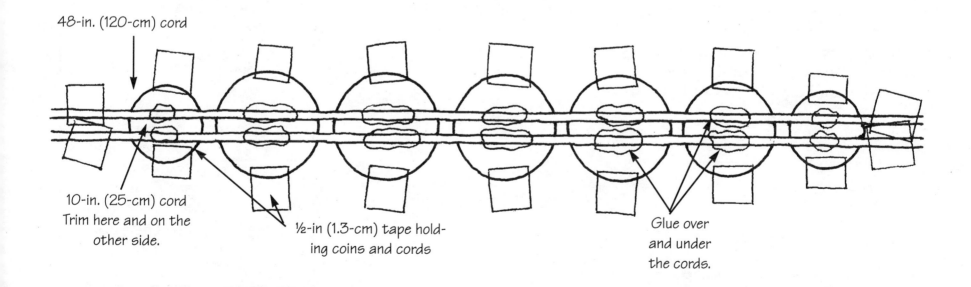

48-in. (120-cm) cord

10-in. (25-cm) cord
Trim here and on the other side.

½-in (1.3-cm) tape holding coins and cords

Glue over and under the cords.

13. Stretch the 10-inch (25-cm) piece of cord above the spots of glue and lower it carefully onto the glue spots. Make sure that the center of the cord is glued to the center coin. Tape each end of the cord to your work surface.

14. Push the cord into each spot of glue. Add a second dab of glue on top of the cord.

15. Place a dab of glue just above the center of each coin.

16. Stretch the 48-inch (1.2-m) piece of cord over the second spots of glue, and lower it carefully onto the glue. Make sure that the center of the cord is glued to the center coin. Tape each end of the cord to your work surface.

17. Push the cord into each spot of glue, and add a second dab of glue on top of the cord. Let the glue dry overnight.

18. Trim the ends of the short cord.

19. Use the long cord to tie the coins around your neck. Trim off any extra cord.

✪ **Even Better:** You can combine this necklace with the Wrapped Earrings on page 83, or with the Ear Decorations on page 25, to make a colorful, recycled ensemble.

Recycling Facts & Tips

Did you know that:

- Recycling isn't really a new idea—people have been doing it for centuries. For example, people have used food scraps to feed animals and make compost to nourish plants since the beginning of history.

How you can help:

- If you have a garden, you can make a compost heap with your food scraps, recycling them into nourishment for the plants. You can build a compost heap by making a container in which you put food scraps, soil, and grass clippings. Ask your parents for help.

Patches

You can make patches for jackets, pants, skirts, backpacks, or whatever you want out of any scraps of cloth. You can customize anything in minutes with these easy, recycled patches.

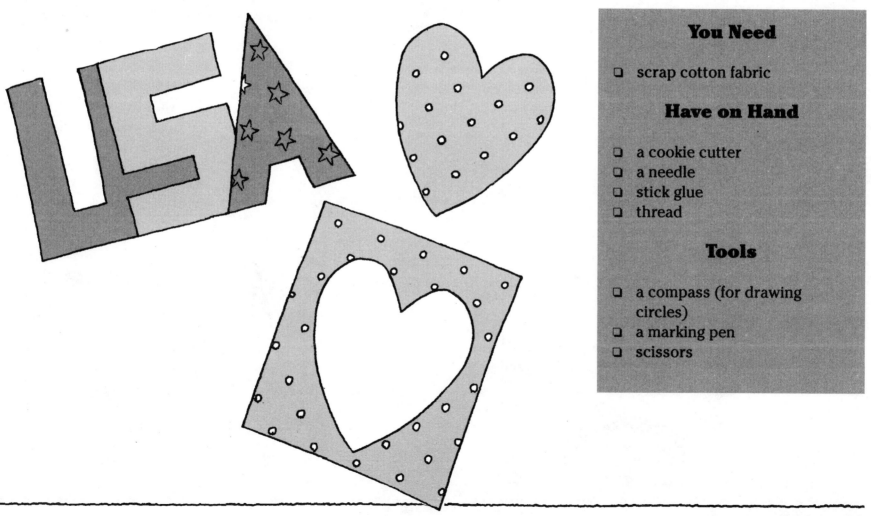

You Need

❑ scrap cotton fabric

Have on Hand

❑ a cookie cutter
❑ a needle
❑ stick glue
❑ thread

Tools

❑ a compass (for drawing circles)
❑ a marking pen
❑ scissors

Instructions

There are three ways to make these patches:

1. Free-hand/cookie cutter:

a. Draw free-hand shapes on the back of a piece of fabric, or trace around the outside of a cookie cutter. You can make one shape, or make several and overlap them.

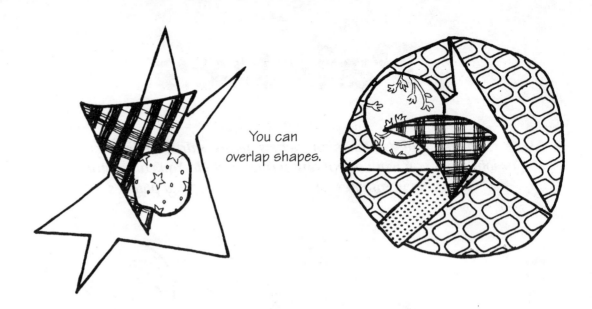

You can overlap shapes.

Trace around a cookie cutter . . .

. . . or make shapes by hand.

b. Cut out the shapes with scissors. See the free-hand patches on this page for some examples.

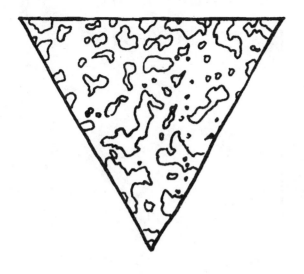

Some patches made with a compass and ruler . . .

2. Compass and ruler:

a. Draw patterns on cardboard with a ruler or compass. Draw circles, squares, or triangles. See the compass and ruler patches on this page for some examples.

b. Cut out the cardboard patterns with scissors.

c. Trace around the patterns onto the back of a piece of fabric.

d. Cut out the outlines with scissors.

. . . and some more.

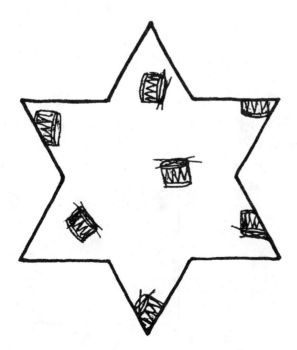

3. Letters and numbers:

a. Measure, mark, and cut out a cardboard rectangle 2¼ × 1½ inches (5.7 × 4 cm).

b. Decide what word you want to spell out—maybe your name. Count the number of letters in the word.

c. Use the cardboard rectangle as a pattern for the letters: Draw one rectangle for each letter onto the back of the fabric.

d. Cut out the fabric rectangles for the letters and numbers. Cut out the shapes of the letters and numbers you want. Don't worry if the letters aren't perfect; they'll look even better if they're all different. Look at the Letter and Number Patterns on pages 69 and 70 for some examples.

There are three ways the patches can be attached:

4. Temporary Patches:

a. Use stick glue on the backs of the patches. (The glue—and the patches—will come off your clothes when you wash them.)

5. Permanent but not washable patches:

a. Use stick glue both on the patches and on the surface they are stuck to.

6. Permanent and washable patches:

a. Use stick glue to hold the patch in place.

b. Sew the edges of the patch to the underlying surface using the Whip Stitch Method (see page 15) and a matching color of thread.

Recycling Facts & Tips

Did you know:

• Rags have been collected to make paper, new cloth, and rugs for hundreds of years. Once they have been collected, the rags are shredded to become the raw fiber for new products.

How you can help:

• You can donate clothing that you have grown out of to charities, such as the Salvation Army. Other products, such as furniture and appliances, can also be donated.

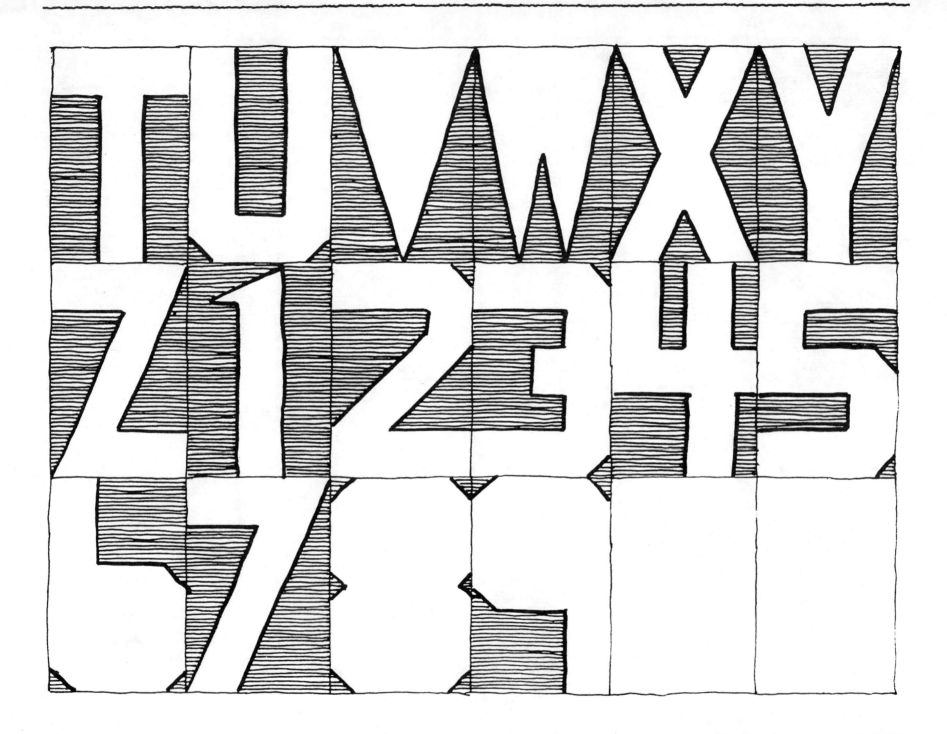

Layered Tops

When a couple of shirts are worn out, you can combine them to make a "hole" new look!

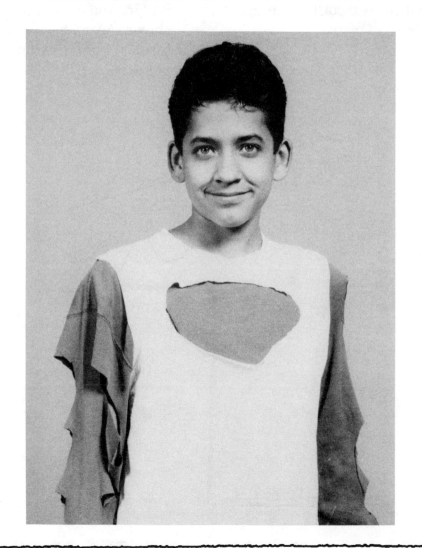

You Need

- ❑ one long-sleeve T-shirt or sweatshirt
- ❑ one short-sleeve T-shirt in a contrasting color

Have on Hand

- ❑ a marking pen

Tools

- ❑ scissors

Instructions:

1. To make the bottom layer:

a. Spread out the long-sleeve shirt and flatten out the sleeves. If the sleeves have cuffs, cut them off.

b. Mark four ovals along one sleeve, as show below.

c. Pinch the fabric inside one of the ovals so that you are holding both the front and back of the sleeve. Cut out the oval, making sure that you are cutting through **both** pieces of cloth.

d. Cut out the other three ovals in the same way.

e. Mark and cut shapes in the other sleeve, as shown in the drawing.

f. Mark and cut the neck hole as shown. Again, be sure to cut through both the front and back of the shirt.

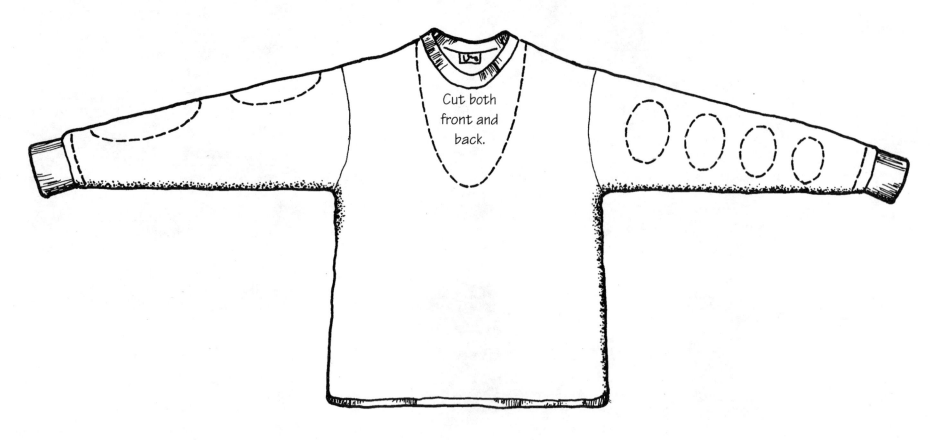

Cut both front and back.

2. To make the top layer:

a. Spread out the short-sleeve T-shirt.

b. Mark and cut out an oval from the front of the T-shirt, as shown. Be sure to cut only through the front piece of fabric.

c. Cut off the sleeves.

d. Cut off the collar, as shown.

3. To wear: Put on the long-sleeve first and then the short-sleeve on top.

✪ **Even Better:** You can decorate the shirts any way you want—by cutting more holes, by drawing on them, or by gluing decorations to them. Be creative!

Cut front only.

Bandanna Shirt

With the help of a needle and thread, you can make this colorful shirt out of four bandannas. When the weather's hot, you'll be cool in this recycled top.

You Need

☐ four colored bandannas, each about 20 inches (50 cm) square
Note: All four bandannas must be the same size.

Have on Hand

☐ a needle
☐ straight pins
☐ thread

Tools

❗ an electric iron
☐ a ruler

Instructions

! 1. Have an **adult helper** iron the bandannas so they are flat (especially the edges).

2. To make the sleeves:

a. Place one bandanna on your work surface and fold it in half, with the fold at the top and the edges at the bottom.

b. Pin the bottom edges together to keep them in place. Sew the edges together using the Whip Stitch Method (see page 15) and remove the pins.

c. Repeat steps **a** and **b** with the second bandanna.

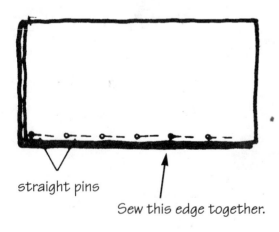

straight pins

Sew this edge together.

4 in. (10 cm)   4 in. (10 cm)

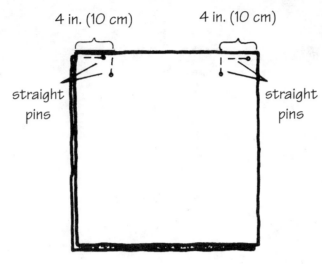

straight pins   straight pins

3. To make the middle:

a. Place the other two bandannas on top of each other. Align the edges and pin them together in two corners.

b. Place pins 4 inches (10 cm) in from each pinned corner to be markers.

c. Sew the edges between the pinned corners and the nearest marker pins together. Remove the pins as you sew. These seams are the shoulders. The space between the stitches is the neck hole.

4. To attach the sleeves:

a. Lay the middle section flat on your work surface. Fold the **front** bandanna up, so it is resting above the back bandanna.

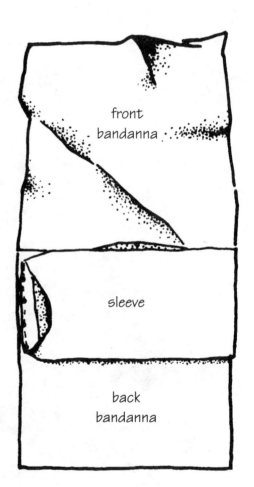

front bandanna

sleeve

back bandanna

b. Turn one sleeve right side out (the sleeves were inside out when you sewed them in step **2**) and lay it across the middle section so that one open end of the sleeve is lined up with one edge of the middle, and the fold of the sleeve is lined up with the shoulder.

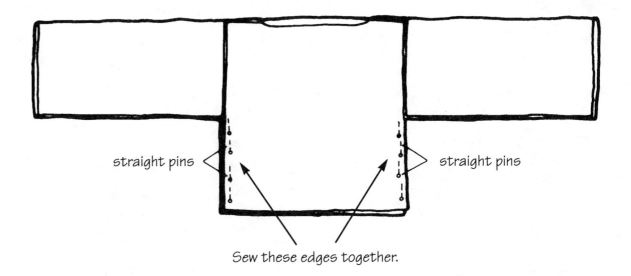

straight pins

straight pins

Sew these edges together.

c. Pin the **back** edge of the sleeve to the back bandanna.

d. Carefully replace the front bandanna over the sleeve.

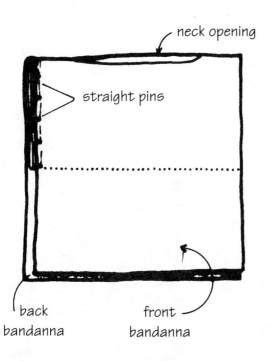

neck opening

straight pins

back bandanna

front bandanna

e. Pin the front edge of the sleeve to the **front** bandanna.

f. Sew each pair of pinned edges together. Remove the pins. Pull the sleeve out.

g. Repeat steps **a–f** to attach the second sleeve on the other side.

5. To sew the side seams:

    a. Pin the front and back bandannas of the middle section together below the sleeves.

    b. Sew the pinned edges together.

6. Turn the shirt right side out and it's ready to wear.

Bar-Code Pin

Turn those boring old bar codes into pins decorated with hot stripes!

You Need

- [ ] several bar-code symbols (such as from boxes or magazines)
  Note: You must get all the bar codes from the same kind of source—all from magazines or all from boxes.
- [ ] 2 × 4½-inch (5 × 11.3-cm) piece of light cardboard,
- [ ] one pin base (You need to buy one at a crafts store.)

Have on Hand

- [ ] a heavy book
- [ ] a pencil
- [ ] stick glue
- [ ] yellow glue

Tools

- [ ] scissors

Instructions

1. Trim the bar codes so that you are left with only the stripes.

2. Place the bar codes onto the cardboard. Arrange the stripes the way you want to wear them (horizontal or vertical).

3. Draw an outline on the cardboard that is slightly larger than the bar codes, as shown.

4. Cut out the outline.

5. Apply stick glue to the cardboard and the back of the bar codes. Glue the bar codes to the cardboard, with the smaller bars of stripes on top of the larger ones.

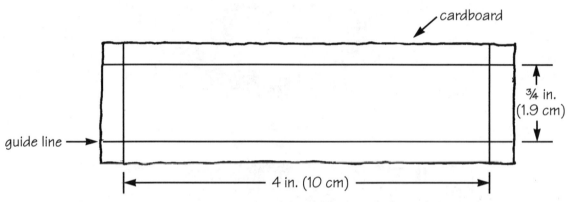

cardboard

guide line →

¾ in. (1.9 cm)

4 in. (10 cm)

Glue bar code pieces to the cardboard along the guide lines
Trim the cardboard to ¾ x 4 in. (2 cm x 10 cm).

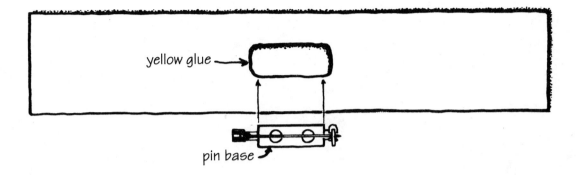

yellow glue

pin base

6. Use the scissors to trim away the extra cardboard around the bar codes.

7. Place a heavy book on top of the cardboard and leave it overnight for the glue to dry.

8. Place a large dab of yellow glue in the center of the back of the cardboard.

9. Press the pin base into the glue.

10. Add more glue on top of the pin base.

Note: Keep the glue away from the pin's moving parts.

11. Let the glue dry overnight.

12. Use your bar-code pin to decorate a coat or shirt, or give pins to your friends.

Foil Necklace

Here's a sparkling set of jewelry you can make from old packing shells and aluminum foil. You can dazzle your friends with your recycled riches.

You Need

- ❏ clean, used aluminum foil
- ❏ shell-shaped Styrofoam packing material
- ❏ heavy black thread

Tools

- ❏ a needle
- ❏ scissors

Instructions

1. Smooth out the aluminum foil and cut it into 3-inch (7.5-cm) squares. You will need 38 squares for a complete matching set.

2. To wrap the shells:

    a. Place the aluminum squares on your work surface, shiny side down.

    b. Place a shell open side up in the middle of the square.

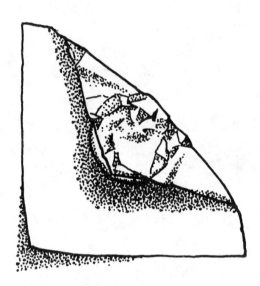

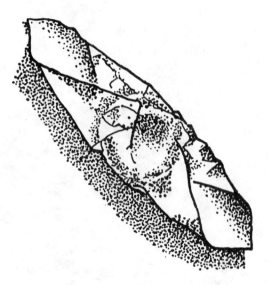

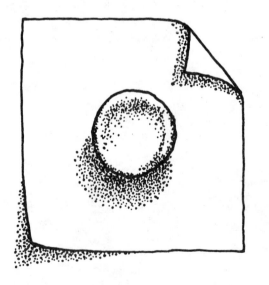

    c. Pull one corner of the foil over the shell and press the foil into the shell.

    d. Press the other three corners into the shell.

    e. Turn the shell over. Gently smooth the foil against the shell inside and outside.

    f. Wrap six shells for each earring. Wrap 26 for the necklace.

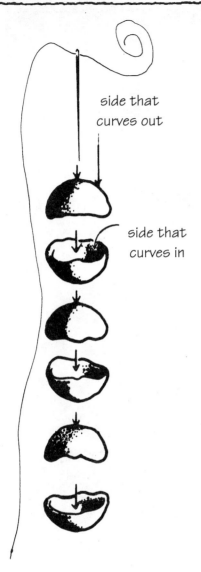

side that
curves out

side that
curves in

b. Carefully push the needle through the center of the side of one shell that curves out. Slide the shell about 24 inches (60 cm) down the thread.

c. Push the needle through the open side of a second shell that curves in. Slide the second shell up against the first.

d. Thread 13 pairs of shells in the same way.

e. Push the shells down the thread so they are 12 inches (30 cm) from the needle.

f. Remove the needle.

g. Tie the ends of the thread together.

4. To make each earring:

a. Thread the needle with a 15-inch (37.5-cm) piece of thread. Make a large knot at the end of the thread.

b. String three pairs of shells as you did for the necklace.

3. To string the necklace:

a. Thread the needle with a 36-inch (90-cm) piece of thread. Tie a knot in the end of the thread.

ear loop

c. Remove the needle and cut the thread.

d. Tie a loop in the end of the thread that is large enough to fit loosely around your ear.

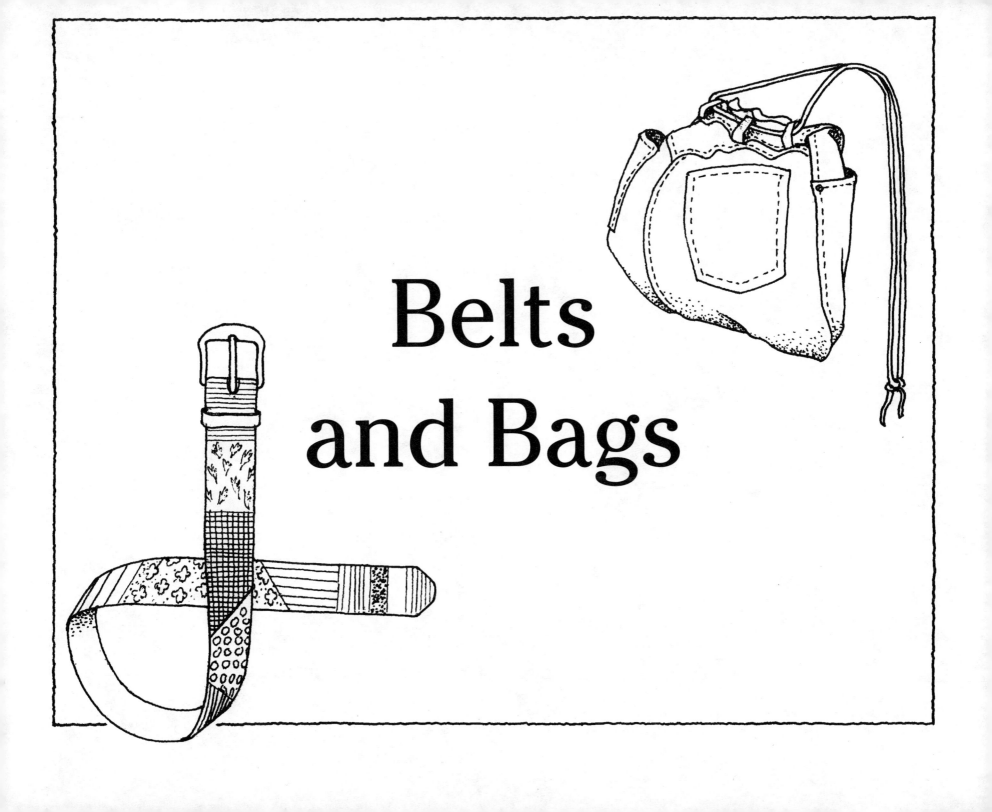

Belts
and Bags

Cloth-Covered Belt

Cover an old leather belt with fabric for the latest in fashion.

You Need

❑ several pieces of fabric with different patterns and colors
❑ an old leather belt that fits you

Have on Hand

❑ stick glue

Tools

❑ scissors
❑ a sharp pencil

Instructions

1. Cut the fabric so that each piece is a little wider than twice the width of the belt. (For example, if your belt is 1 inch [2.5 cm] wide, your fabric should be a little more than 2 inches [5 cm] wide.) Vary the fabric lengths from 3 to 5 inches (7.5-12.5 cm).

2. Lay the belt flat on your work surface.

3. To glue the first piece of fabric:

    a. Hold one of the pieces of fabric up to the belt. Starting at the end of the belt opposite the buckle, apply stick glue to the front of the belt for a little more than the length of the piece of fabric. Also apply stick glue to the back of the piece of fabric.

    b. Place the middle of the glued side of the fabric down on the glued side of the belt, so that 1½ inches (4 cm) of fabric extend beyond the end of the belt. Smooth the fabric down with your fingers.

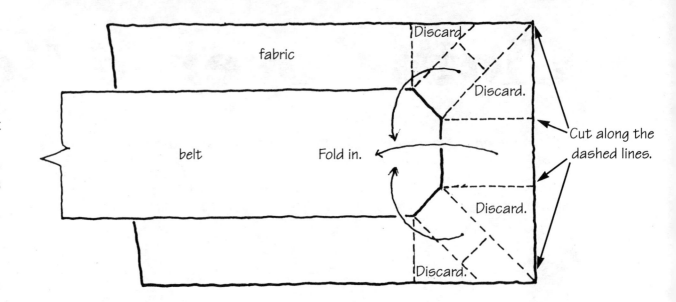

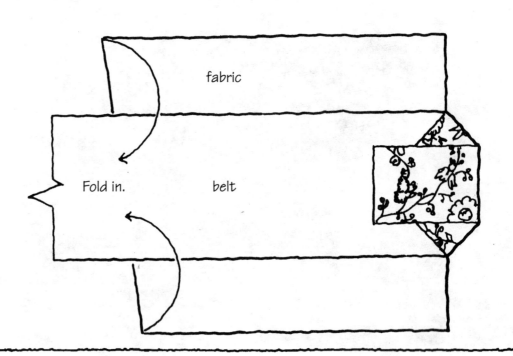

c. Turn the belt over. Cut the fabric that extends beyond the end of the belt, as shown in the drawing on the opposite page.

d. Apply glue to the back of the belt and to the fabric.

e. Wrap the fabric around the end of the belt. Smooth out any wrinkles.

4. To glue the middle pieces of fabric:

a. Apply stick glue to the belt and to the back of each piece of fabric.

b. Place each piece of fabric on the belt, overlapping the edge of the piece already glued in place by ½ inch (1.3 cm). Wrap each piece of fabric around the belt. Smooth out any wrinkles.

c. Continue to add pieces of fabric until you are about ½ inch (1.3 cm) away from the buckle.

5. To glue the last piece of fabric:

a. Cut a square piece of fabric exactly the size of the belt width. For example, if your belt is 1 inch (2.5 cm) wide, the fabric should be 1 inch (2.5 cm) square.

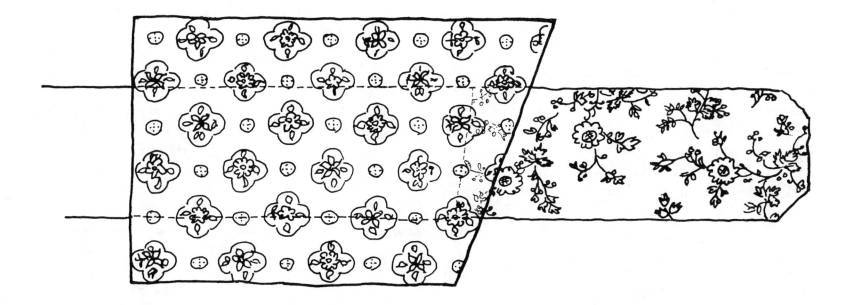

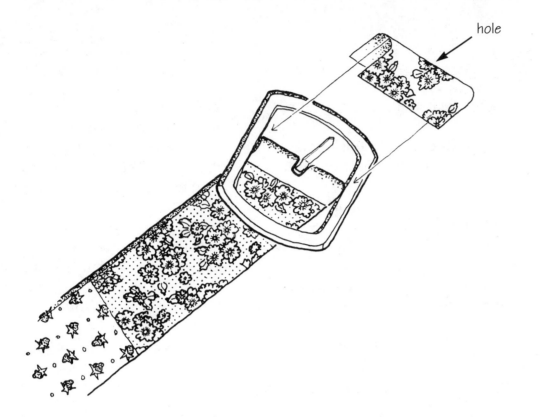

hole

b. Use a sharp pencil to carefully poke a hole in the center of the fabric.

c. Apply glue to the back of the fabric and to the front and back of the belt end near the buckle.

d. Place the buckle tongue through the hole in the fabric and press the fabric against the end of the belt. Smooth out the fabric, and make sure the edges are even with the belt.

6. Use the pencil point to open the belt holes in the fabric.

7. Slip your belt on and buckle it up!

Yarn Belt

*You can make this colorful belt from leftover yarn,
or you can unravel an old sweater!*

You Need

- ❑ yarn in three colors: 40 feet (12 m) each of two colors, and 20 feet (6 m) of a third color

Note: If you use unraveled yarn from a sweater, be sure to wet it first, pat it dry in a towel, and hang it to dry. This will take out the "kinks."

Have on Hand

- ❑ two chairs
- ❑ a marking pen
- ❑ masking tape
- ❑ some extra scrap yarn

Tools

- ❑ a ruler
- ❑ scissors

Instructions

1. Wrap a piece of yarn around your waist. Mark where the yarn overlaps.

2. Lay the yarn on your work surface.

3. Measure and mark a point that is 2 feet (60 cm) from the first point you marked. Cut the yarn at the second mark.

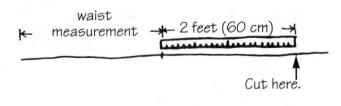

waist measurement — 2 feet (60 cm) →

Cut here.

4. Place the two chairs back to back. They should be slightly apart, so that you can wrap the piece of yarn you cut in step **3** once around them both. When you have placed the chairs correctly, discard this piece of yarn.

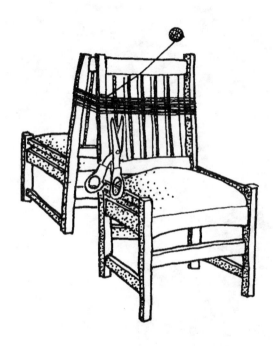

5. To wrap the belt:

a. Tape one end of one 40-foot (12-meter) piece of yarn to one of the chairs.

b. Wrap the yarn around both chairs 10 times. When you have finished the last wrap, use scissors to cut through all the wraps at once.

c. Carefully place the yarn on a flat surface out of the way.

d. Repeat steps **a–c** with each of the remaining colors. Make 10 wraps of the second color and four wraps of the third color.

e. Lay all three bunches of yarn together, with the strands at one end lined up. If the other end of the bunches looks ragged, even it off with scissors, as shown below.

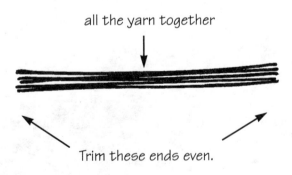

all the yarn together

Trim these ends even.

6. To finish the belt:

a. Cut a 15-inch (38-cm) -long piece from the scrap yarn.

b. Measure and mark a point 12 inches (30 cm) from one end of the bunch of yarn, as shown below.

c. Tie the piece of yarn you have just cut around the point you have marked. Wrap the remainder tightly around the three bunches of yarn, as shown at right. Tie the two ends of the short piece of yarn together.

d. Repeat steps **a–c** at the other end of the three bunches of yarn.

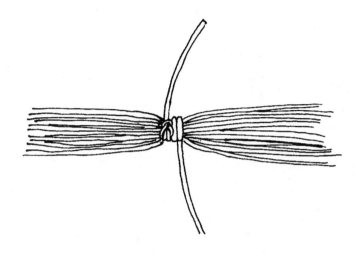

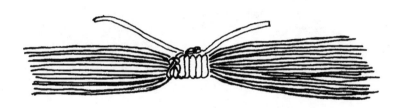

|← 12 in. →|←— waist measurement —→|← 12 in. →|
| (30 cm) | | (30 cm) |

7. Place the finished belt around your waist. Tie the ends of the belt together.

Tote Bag

Don't throw away that old, ripped-up pair of jeans; make them into a carry-all instead.

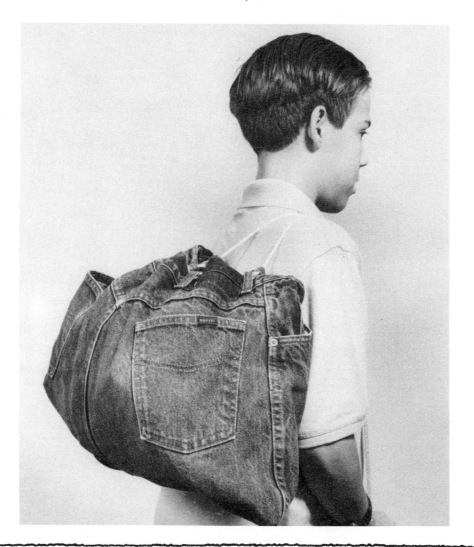

You Need

- an old, clean pair of adult jeans

Note: Use a pair of kid-sized jeans to make a smaller bag.

- about 60 inches (1.5 m) of soft rope

Have on Hand

- a marking pen
- a ruler
- straight pins
- strong thread

Tools

- a needle
- ! sharp fabric scissors

Instructions

1. Button or zip up the jeans, and turn them inside out.

2. Lay the jeans on the floor. Smooth out one leg.

3. Place the ruler at the crotch of the jeans and across one leg (the placement doesn't have to be exact). Use the marking pen to draw a guide line across the leg.

4. Measure two points on the leg that are 1½ inch (4 cm) below the first line. Use the ruler and the marking pen to draw a line connecting these two points. This line will be the cutting line.

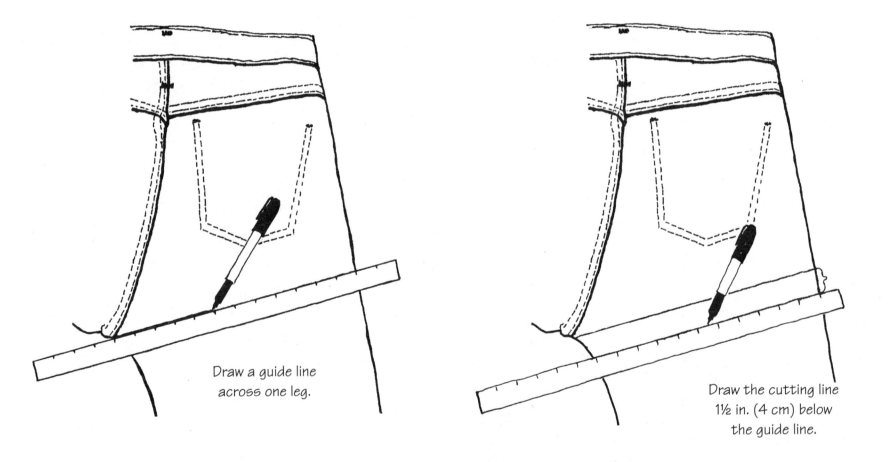

Draw a guide line across one leg.

Draw the cutting line 1½ in. (4 cm) below the guide line.

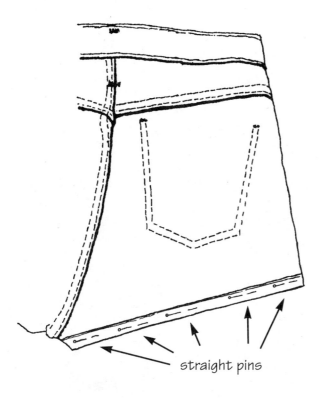

Fold the bottom edge up to the guide line. Pin the edge in several places.

straight pins

8. Sew the folds of each leg together using the Whip Stitch Method (see page 15). Keep the stitches close together, and about ¼ inch (.6 cm) long, so the seam will be strong. Remove the pins as you sew.

9. Turn the jeans right side out. Push the corners of the seams out.

10. Thread the rope through the belt loops. Tie the ends of the rope together to make a strap.

✪ **Even Better:** Decorate your bag with the Patches on page 65.

! 5. Have an **adult helper** use the sharp scissors to cut along the cutting line. Make sure to cut through both the front and back of the pants leg, but not through the pockets.

6. Repeat steps **3–5** for the other leg.

7. Fold the bottom edge of each leg up to the first line you drew. Pin the folded edge to the jeans in several places.

Plastic-Bag Belt

Instead of throwing away those bags from the dry cleaners, you can turn them into a unique belt.

Instructions

1. Remove any tags or labels from the bags.

2. Cut several pieces of masking tape about 3 inches (7.5 cm) long. Stick them on the edge of your work surface, so they're ready when you need them.

3. Bunch the bags together by pulling them through your hand.

Wrap masking tape around the bags at points 3 in. (7.5 cm) from the middle.

6. Wrap pieces of masking tape around the bags at the points you marked in step **5** (not in the middle).

7. Starting from one of the taped points, measure and tape points every 6 inches (15 cm) along the bags, until you are 6 to 8 inches (15–20 cm) from the end. Leave the end loose.

8. Repeat step **7** on the other side of the belt.

Bunch the bags together by pulling them through your hand.

4. Use the ruler and marking pen to measure and mark the exact middle of the bags.

5. Measure and mark points 3 inches (7.5 cm) on either side of the middle.

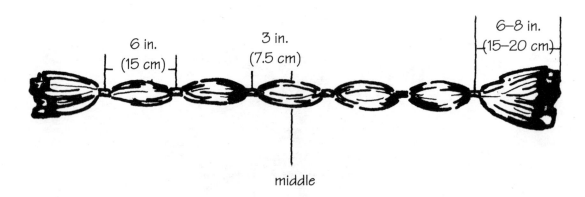

6 in. (15 cm)

3 in. (7.5 cm)

6–8 in. (15–20 cm)

middle

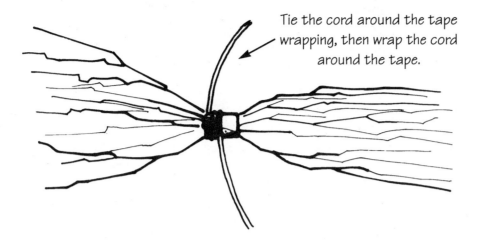

Tie the cord around the tape wrapping, then wrap the cord around the tape.

9. Cut pieces of cord that are 18 inches (45 cm) long for each of the tape wrappings **except** the two ends. Tie these cords around the inner tape wrappings, then wrap the cord around the tape. When you have covered the entire tape wrapping, tie the ends of the cord together. Use scissors to trim off any extra cord.

10. Cut two pieces of cord that are 30 inches (75 cm) long for the tape wrappings on the ends. Tie these cords to the tape wrappings nearest the ends. Use the ends of these cords to tie the belt around your waist.

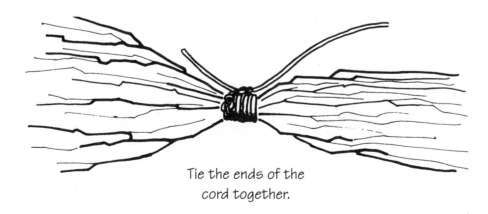

Tie the ends of the cord together.

Recycling Tips & Facts

Did you know that:

- Recycling steel takes several steps. After the used steel is collected, it's taken to a processing center, where a huge magnet is used to separate steel cans from the rest of the recyclables. The cans are packed into large bales and shipped to a steel plant, where they are melted down and made into new products.

How you can help:

- Be sure to rinse your recyclable cans and bottles. Many cities also suggest that you remove the labels.

Stuff for Your Hands & Feet

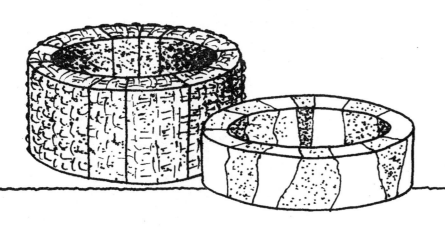

Spiral Bracelet

This wraparound made from a toilet-paper tube and foil goes with anything. It can be formal jewelry, or it can be part of an interstellar uniform.

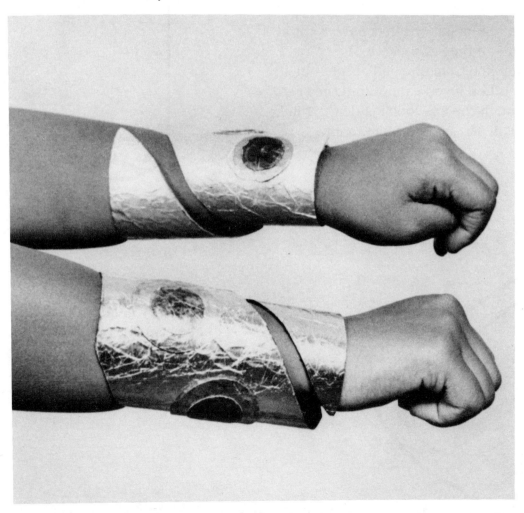

Instructions

1. Crumple the foil into a loose ball to give it texture. Carefully uncrumple the foil and smooth it out.

2. Coat the back of the foil **and** the outside of the toilet-paper tube with stick glue.

3. Place the foil on your work surface with the glue side up, and the short end toward you. Place the tube lengthwise along the long edge of the foil. Roll the tube onto the foil. Smooth down any wrinkles.

4. Overlap the foil about ¼ inch (0.6 cm). Trim away all the extra foil.

5. All toilet-paper tubes have a spiral seam on them. Cut along the spiral seam line from one end of the tube to the other. If you cannot find the seam through the foil, look inside the tube so you can see the seam to cut.

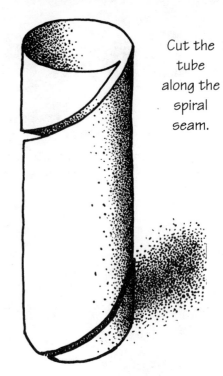

Cut the tube along the spiral seam.

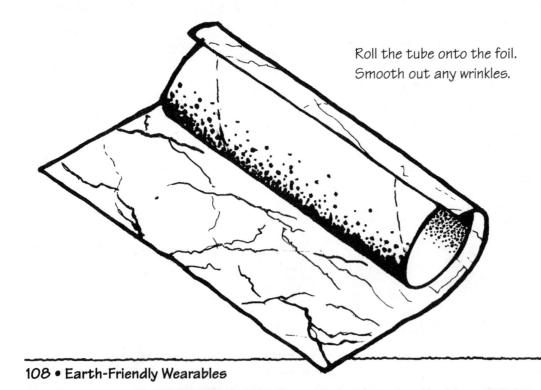

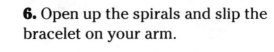

Roll the tube onto the foil. Smooth out any wrinkles.

6. Open up the spirals and slip the bracelet on your arm.

✪ **Even Better:** You can decorate the bracelet by gluing on cardboard shapes, such as small circles, squares, and triangles cut from another toilet-paper tube. You can color these shapes or cover them with foil.

Rings

Scrap cardboard and pictures from magazines can quickly become recycled treasure. With rings this fun and easy to make, you'll want to wear one on every finger!

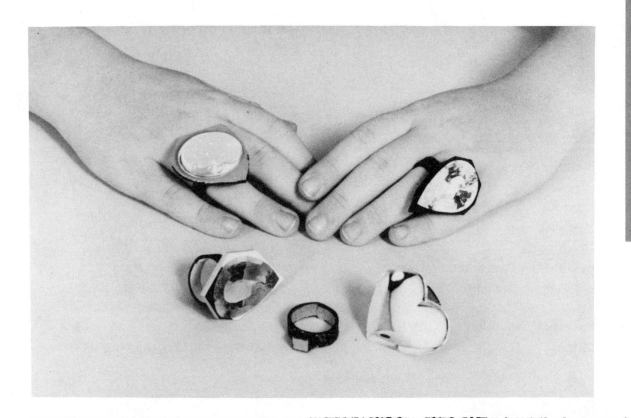

You Need

❑ light cardboard (such as from a cookie or cracker box)
❑ life-size photos of gems cut from magazines or catalogs

Have on Hand

❑ stick glue
❑ transparent tape
❑ white glue

Tools

❑ a pencil
❑ a ruler
❑ scissors
❑ a spring clothespin

Instructions

1. Cut a cardboard strip ¼ inch (.6 cm) wide and about 8 inches (20 cm) long.

2. Wrap the strip around your ring finger and mark where the strip overlaps. Cut the strip at that mark.

3. Curl the cardboard into a band. Use a piece of tape to hold the ends together, as shown.

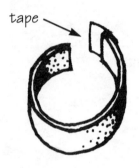

tape →

first piece of cardboard

4. Try on the band for fit. If it is too big, cut it slightly shorter. If it is too small, discard it and cut a new strip that is slightly longer.

5. Cut a strip of cardboard long enough to fit around the first band.

6. Glue the second band around the first with white glue. The ends of the bands should be on opposite sides. Use the clothespin to hold the second band in place for about 20 minutes while the glue dries.

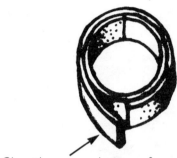

Glue the second piece of cardboard to the first.

7. Cut two pieces of cardboard ¼ inch (.6 cm) wide and ¼ inch (.6 cm) long and one piece of cardboard ¼ inch (.6 cm) wide and ³⁄₈ inch (1 cm) long.

8. Glue the two ¼-inch (.6-cm) -square pieces together.

9. Glue these pieces to the third piece.

10. Glue the other side of the ³⁄₈-inch (1-cm) piece to the band. Make sure it goes across the seam.

11. Attach the cut-out photo to a flat piece of cardboard with stick glue. Trim the cardboard to whatever shape you want.

12. Apply white glue to the back of the cardboard with the picture on it, and to the top ¼-inch (.6-cm) piece on the ring setting. Carefully center the image and press it onto the setting.

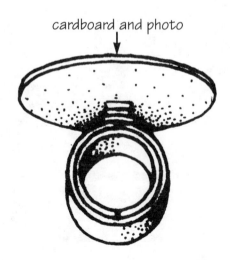

cardboard and photo

13. Let the ring dry overnight.

Fancy Shoelaces

Jazz up your footwear with shoelaces of many colors.
Make different-colored laces for each shoe!

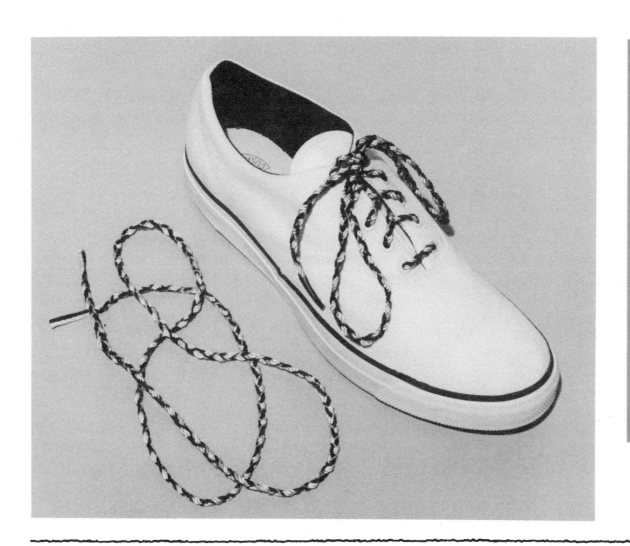

You Need

❏ two 60-inch (150-cm) pieces of string (you can color them with a marker)
❏ two 60-inch (150-cm) pieces of thin black cord (such as gift-wrap cord)
❏ two 60-inch (150-cm) pieces of medium-thickness cord

Note: Make sure the cords and string are thin enough to fit through your shoe eyelets **together** before you start to braid.

(continued on the next page)

Have on Hand

- ❏ a short piece of scrap cord or string
- ❏ transparent tape
- ❏ white glue

Tools

- ❏ a ruler
- ❏ scissors
- ❏ two spring clothespins

Instructions

1. Lay the cords and string out so that their ends are even. Tie them together at one end.

2. Tie the piece of scrap cord around the end of the tied-together cords and string, below the knot. Tie the other end of this scrap cord to a doorknob, so that the tied-together strings and cords stay taut as you braid.

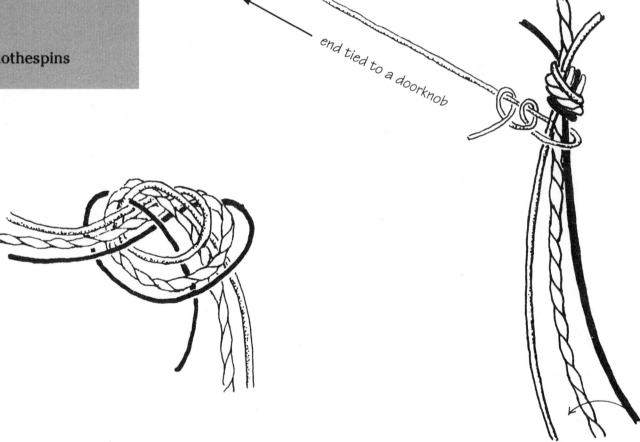

end tied to a doorknob

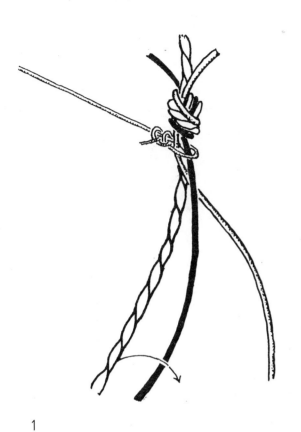

1

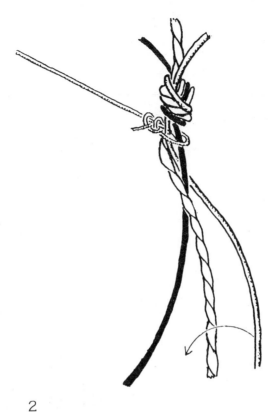

2

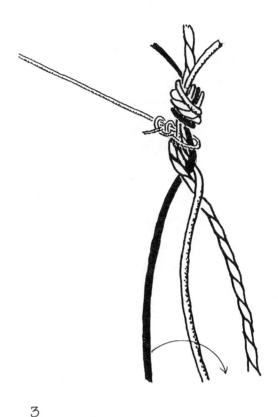

3

3. If you don't already know how to braid, follow these instructions.

a. Begin by holding two cords in your right hand and one in your left.

b. Place the left cord **over** the center cord and take the center cord into your left hand. You now have two cords in your right hand.

c. Place the right cord **over** the center cord and take the center cord into your right hand. You now have two cords in your right hand.

4. Continue to braid until you are about 2 inches (5 cm) from the loose end of the cords and string. Clamp the end of the braid with a clothespin.

Note: If you need to stop before you have finished the braid, clamp the part you have finished with a clothespin.

5. Untie the braid from the doorknob.

6. Untie the knot at the beginning of the braid. Clamp this end of the braid with a clothespin.

7. Measure the shoelaces in your shoes against the braid. Trim the braid so that it is the same length as your shoelace. Put a clothespin on the braid to hold it together while you cut.

8. Apply glue along the cords for 1 inch (2.5 cm) at both ends of the braid and press the cords together to make stiff tips. Hold the cords at each end in place by wrapping a piece of transparent tape just below the glue.

9. Allow the glue to dry for two hours. Trim the lace at the ends.

10. Repeat to make the second shoelace.

Four Bracelets

You can use all the colors of the rainbow to make bracelets out of ribbon spools and some scraps of foil or yarn. Here are four different kinds of bracelet you can make.

You Need

- a plastic gift-wrap ribbon spool (that fits on your wrist)
- gold and silver foil (from chocolate bars)
- knitting yarn

Have on Hand

- colored pencils or crayons
- a comb
- marking pens
- masking tape
- tape
- white glue
- white paper

Tools

- a glue brush
- a large-eyed tapestry needle
- scissors
- a spring clothespin

Instructions

1. Wrap the spool inside and out with masking tape. This will form the base of the bracelet.

Decorate the bracelet using one of these 4 methods:

2. Decorating with gold and silver foil:

a. Clean the foil with a damp cloth.

b. Tear the foil into strips ¾ inch (2 cm) wide and twice as long as the bracelet is wide.

c. Brush glue onto the back of each strip of foil.

d. Wrap each strip around the bracelet, overlapping until the whole bracelet is covered.

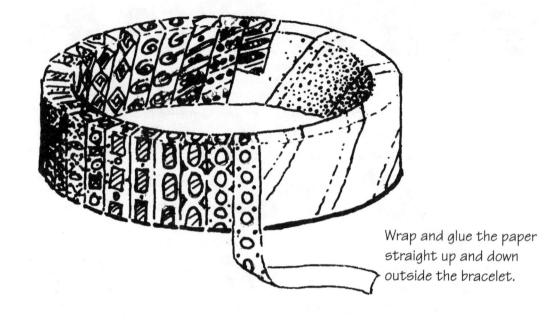

Wrap and glue the paper straight up and down outside the bracelet.

3. Using decorated paper:

a. Cut strips of paper about ¼ inch (.6 cm) wide and 10 inches (25 cm) long.

b. Decorate the strips of paper using crayons, colored pencils, or marking pens.

c. Coat the backs of the strips with glue. Wrap the strips around the bracelet the short way (see above), so that they overlap slightly.

d. When the paper has dried, brush a thin coat of glue over the entire bracelet.

4. Wrapping with yarn:

a. Tie together differently colored pieces of yarn to make a piece about 4 feet (1.2 m) long.

b. Glue one end of the yarn to the inside of the bracelet. Use a piece of tape to hold the yarn in place while the glue dries. It's OK to go on to the next step before the glue is dry.

c. Wrap the yarn around the bracelet the short way.

d. Make sure the wraps touch but don't overlap, so that none of the bracelet shows through.

Note: If the yarn is too short, use a spring clothespin to hold the wraps in place while you tie more yarn onto the loose end.

e. When the bracelet is almost completely wrapped, spread glue on the surface and lay the last few wraps in the glue. Use tape to hold down the wraps until the glue dries completely.

f. Once the glue is dry, trim off any extra yarn.

5. Wrapping and weaving with yarn:

a. Find or tie together a piece of yarn about 4 feet (1.2 m) long.

b. Loosely wrap the first piece of yarn around the bracelet the short way. This is similar to the wrapping in step **4**, but should be much looser.

c. Thread the second piece of yarn onto the needle.

d. Start weaving at the top of the bracelet, placing the needle over and under the wraps.

e. Pull the yarn tight after each circuit around the bracelet. After you have gone around a few times, push the weaves together using the teeth of a comb.

f. The last few weaves will become very tight. When you are finished, cut off any excess yarn.

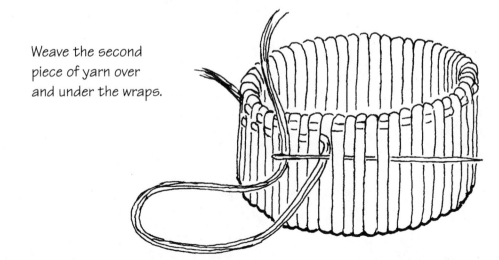

Weave the second piece of yarn over and under the wraps.

Cloth Fingernails

Funky fingernails finalize your fashions!
Scrap cloth and false fingernails
quickly become the latest thing.

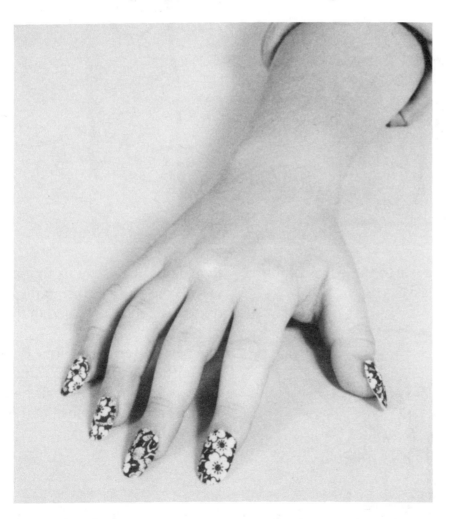

Instructions

1. Use the fingernail clipper to trim the false nails to fit your nails. Use the nail file to round and smooth the edges.

2. Cut 10 pieces of fabric that are a little larger than your fingernails.

3. Roughen the surface of the false nails with the nail file so the glue will stick better.

4. Rub stick glue on both the false nails and the back of each piece of fabric, one at a time. Place the fabric on the nail. Press the fabric and the nails firmly together so there are no wrinkles or bubbles.

5. Trim the fabric to the edges of the nails with the scissors.

double-sided tape

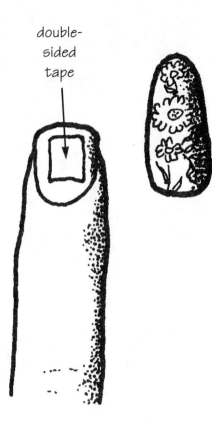

6. Attach the false nails to your nails with ½-inch (1.3-cm) squares of double-sided tape folded in half.

✪ **Even Better:** Make your Cloth Fingernails out of the same cloth as your favorite shirt or pants and you can have a coordinated ensemble.

Mosaic Fingernails

Fashionable fake fingernails can be made from simple eggshells.

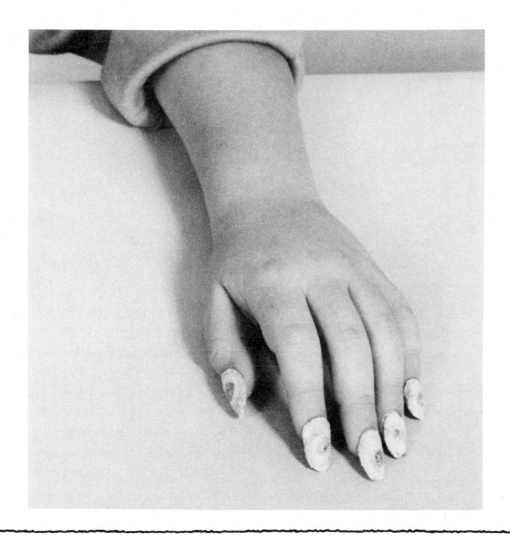

You Need

- ❑ four eggshells
- ❑ a set of false fingernails
  (You need to buy these.)

Have on Hand

- ❑ a dinner plate
- ❑ dishwashing detergent
- ❑ double-sided tape
- ❑ marking pens in several colors
- ❑ soft, clean rags
- ❑ white glue

Tools

- ❑ a fingernail clipper
- ❑ a nail file

Instructions

1. Use the nail clipper to trim the false nails to fit your nails. Use the nail file to round and smooth the edges.

2. Carefully wash the insides of the eggshells using a couple of drops of dishwashing detergent in water. Gently dry the eggshells with soft, clean rags.

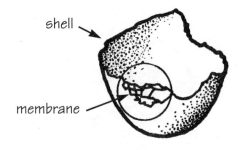

At places like the area circled, grasp the membrane and broken shell to pull the membrane out of the shell.

3. Pick away the membranes that line the insides of the shells.

4. Break the eggshells into 10 pieces, each larger than a fingernail.

5. Decorate each of the pieces of shell with marking pens.

6. Squeeze out a drop of glue about the size of a dime onto the plate.

7. Place one of the eggshell pieces on top of the drop of glue, with the decorated side up. Carefully press the shell into the glue, breaking the shell into many smaller pieces. Make sure that the pieces don't scatter.

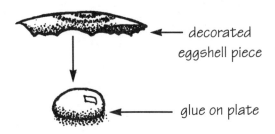

decorated eggshell piece

glue on plate

Note: The glue **must** spread beyond the edges of the shell pieces. If it doesn't, add more glue at the edges.

8. Repeat steps **6** and **7** for the other nine shell pieces.

9. Allow the shells and glue to stand undisturbed 8 to 12 hours.

10. Pick at the edges of the glue until you can peel the glue and all of the shell in one piece from the plate. The glue under the shells will still be wet.

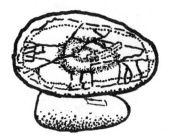

eggshell with glue hardened around its outside edges lifted from the plates

Press it and the false fingernail together.

11. Place the mosaic shell bits and the glue onto the false nails. Press the shells firmly onto the nails.

12. Let the glue dry overnight. Trim the excess mosaic shell from the edges of the nails with the clipper.

13. Attach the false nails to your nails with ½ inch (1.3 cm) squares of double-sided tape folded in half.

Figure-Eight Bracelet

Packing materials can be easily transformed into terrific jewelry. Here you can use Styrofoam figure-eights to stylishly package your wrist.

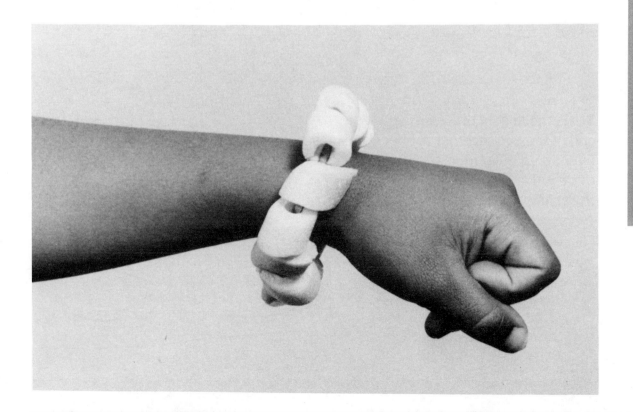

Instructions

1. Use the scissors to cut each piece of Styrofoam in half at the middle, so you have 12 small ovals.

Cut along the line.

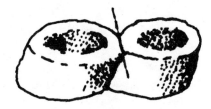

Rubber bands

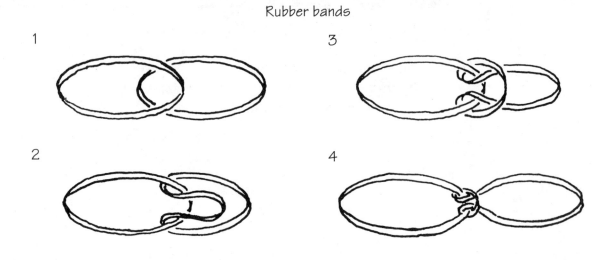

2. Link the rubber bands together by placing one rubber band on top of the other and pulling one end of the bottom rubber band through and over the top rubber band and through the center of itself. Pull the rubber bands tight.

3. Tie the middle of the string to one end of the tied-together rubber bands, by looping the middle around a rubber band and pulling the ends of the string through the loop.

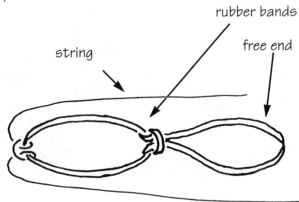

string

rubber bands

free end

Open a paper clip.

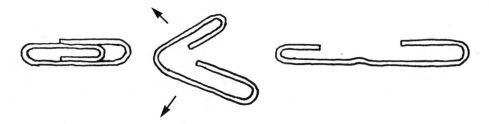

9. Cut off the excess string with the scissors.

4. Straighten out the paper clip so you have a hook on each end.

5. Hook the free end of the rubber bands over one end of the paper clip.

6. Gently push the paper clip and rubber bands through the center of each Styrofoam oval, so that all 12 ovals are threaded onto the rubber bands.

7. Unhook the paper clip.

8. Slip one end of the string through the free end of the rubber bands. Bring the ends of the rubber bands together and tie the string to hold them tightly together.

10. Slip the finished bracelet over your wrist.

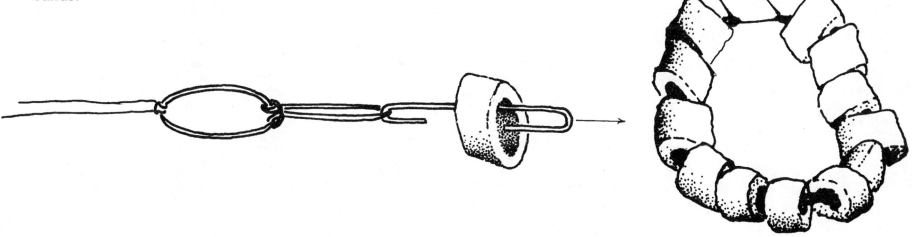

Staying Earth-Friendly

In this book there are facts and tips about trash, recycling, and how you can help save the Earth.

If you want more information about how you can help, you can write to the groups listed here. These organizations can give you ideas and information about reducing, reusing, and recycling.

Don't forget about your local resources. Parents, teachers, neighbors, and friends probably have lots of information about how your community recycles.

Organizations

Coalition for a Recyclable Waste Stream
1525 New Hampshire Ave., NW
Washington, DC 20036
(301) 891-1100

The Environmental Action Coalition
625 Broadway, Second Floor
New York, NY 10012
(212) 677-1601

Environmental Defense Fund
475 Park Ave. South
New York, NY 10016
(800) CALL-EDF

Inform
381 Park Ave. South
New York, NY 10016
(212) 689-4040

Keep America Beautiful
Mill River Plaza
9 West Broad St.
Stamford, CT 06902
(203) 323-8987

National Recycling Coalition
1101 30th St., NW
Washington, DC 20007
(202) 625-6406

Natural Resource Defense Council
40 West 20th St.
New York, NY 10011
(212) 727-2700

Other Books

If you've enjoyed reading Earth-Friendly Wearables, you might also enjoy these books:

About Garbage and Stuff.
Ann A. Shanks, Viking Press,
New York, 1973.

Cartons, Cans, and Orange Peels: Where Does Your Garbage Go?
Joanna Foster, Clarion Books,
New York, 1991.

Earth Book for Kids: Activities to Help Heal the Environment.
Linda Schwartz, The Learning Works,
Santa Barbara, Calif., 1990.

The Kid's Guide to Social Action.
Barbara A. Lewis, Free Spirit
Publishing, Minneapolis, 1991.

The Lorax. Dr. Seuss,
Random House, New York, 1988.

Taking Out the Trash: A No-Nonsense Guide to Recycling.
Jennifer Carfess, Island Press,
Washington, D.C., 1992.